# Treasure
# From The
# Master's Heart

Gregory R Reid

# FOREWORD

This book was born out of my love for the devotional books of Oswald Chambers and, especially, Amy Carmichael. I began writing personal insights into scripture in my morning devotional time, beginning in 1981. Years later it is being published. Many profound personal changes have taken place in my life since I first began writing this, and the struggles and joys have just deepened my confidence in the strength and insight the Lord gave me in the writing. Final additions were added this year, to complete a 365-day devotional book.

The scriptures are most helpful when they become personal. I hope this book makes His Word personal to you and encourages you to dig deeper in your own quest for intimacy with the Father. Let His Word dwell in you richly and root downward into all that you are and have.

Gregory R Reid
March 2019

For Julian - Who asked for the Treasure,
And asks for it still.

## DEDICATION

To all my spiritual parents that helped raise me to love Jesus, love God's Word, and love His ways: Doris Shumate, Dave and Jan Malkin, Claudette Stewart and Rosemary Beugler, Mom Shirley Davis, Audrey and Charles Meier, Rick and Anita Howard, Nick and Lenore Lengyel, and the ones who took me in as their second boy, Ken and Marlys Upke. I pray all your love and prayers for me have borne fruit to the glory of Jesus and the blessing of His people, and that this book reflects the pouring out you did in my life.

# January 1ˢᵗ
## Business

"Ponder the path of your feet, and let all your ways be established." Proverbs 4:26

Busy days, endless tasks and appointments. Then slowly you start to realize: I don't know where I'm going. I don't even know where I am, or how I got here. You've scheduled God out of your life, and with Him, that surety of His guiding hand. It is an act of His love that you've become aimless. Now stop, wait. Ponder your foot's path; how much busy-work is just that? Re-arrange priorities: give God the tithe, the first fruit, the best of your time. How did you get here?

And ahead - plan God into every move. Take time to look hard at your footsteps, past, current and future: lay all down at His cross and pray, "O God, here are my plans. Now show me what you want me to do."

# January 2<sup>nd</sup>
## Words

"Set a watch, Lord, before my mouth; keep the door of my lips." Psalms 141:3

Much grief could be avoided by making this a daily prayer. Invite the Holy Spirit to guard your mouth and check your words. You'll be shocked at how much of your conversation cuts, tears, destroys, hurts, burns. When the Watchman checks your words and convicts you to be silent, then ask that He may put His words into your mouth, that you can speak words of gentleness, truth, kindness, encouragement, and hope.

"Let no corrupt communication proceed out of your mouth but that which is good to the use of edifying, that it may minister grace unto the hearer." Ephesians 4:29

# January 3rd
## Timing

"My times are in Thy hand." Psalms 31:15a

Never forget that the Eternal One is timeless; He is neither rushed nor a slow worker. Because He sees time from beginning to end, He is able to work free of the burdens of too little and too much time we humans are often enslaved to.

Have you waited for His will and direction a long and agonizing time? Trust Him: He has not forgotten; your times are in His hands. Are you hurried, rushed, filled with anxiousness and urgency? Slow down: trust Him who never panics; your times are in His hands. When we cease playing God with our time, we can rest in Him who works all according to His will and take no thought for tomorrow.

# January 4<sup>th</sup>
## Paradox

"As sorrowful, yet always rejoicing." 2 Corinthians 6:10

This is one of the great paradoxes of our faith. A believer can be joyous while sad, sad even though rejoicing. The heart may be breaking due to hard trials, broken relationships, tremendous fires, and yet our faces plainly evidence the reality of Romans 8:28: "We know it's working for our good." On the edge of pain, we learn that God is master of all our times; all our circumstances. The Bible neither preaches a stoic type of grim-faced endurance nor a happy-hallelujah kind of "grin and bear it" attitude. Instead, it teaches us to experience the pain, because it produces positive things: endurance, character, hope, the love of God. Because we know that, then we can smile and even laugh in the face of trials, the kind that says, "I've got a secret." That secret is that God is making gold, and making us sweeter, freer, more loving and compassionate. We do not deny the pain. We merely acknowledge and rejoice by faith in its perfecting results.

# January 5ᵗʰ
## Search

"...They received the word with all readiness of mind, and searched the Scriptures daily, whether those things were so." Acts 17:11

The Bereans were commended as noble by God. They did not just receive the Word. They received it with a ready mind. Not only so, but they searched the Scriptures daily to verify what they heard. In this age of pseudo-teachers and false prophets, how much we need the Berean spirit. So often, like baby birds, we open our hungry mouths to be spiritually fed, swallowing anything, from worm to razor blade. Caution is an unpopular word in our fellowship of seminars, conventions and home groups. Deception is rampant. Why? The key to the Bereans' spiritual success lies in this: they daily searched the Scriptures. When we stop blindly accepting every teaching as from God because someone uses the Name of Jesus, when we begin to study the Word of God every day, then we will not be deceived.

# January 6<sup>th</sup>
## Plowing

"Doth the plowman plow all day to sow?" Isaiah 28:24a)

In the summer of our harvest, how blessed we are with bountiful grain! But old crops rot and must be plowed under for the long winter, awaiting the season of new sowing. Has your "plowing" been long and severe? Have you felt the agony of barren ground? Is the Word dry, are your prayers going seemingly unanswered? Fear not, barren one! Though the plowing seems long and painful. He will once more sow and plant for the New Harvest in your life! The longer the winter, the deeper the plowing, the greater harvest of ministry will come in your spring.

"In due season we shall reap, if we faint not." (Galatians 6:9b)

# January 7th
# Princes

"...That He may set him with princes..." Psalms 113:8

If only we could fully comprehend what this means. He has taken us out of our rags, out of the garbage heap, and elevated us to Princehood. How different our behavior would be! How different our attitude about ourselves, about others, about our Father-King, and especially our role and position in life. Our heads would be lifted higher, our steps surer and yet more careful, our love toward others more responsible. You can easily "act" like you are a Prince, a "King's kid" - and you may well be. But one who really knows their Princehood will not flaunt it proudly; rather they will carry that title humbly, and with great, quiet confidence. They do not talk their authority - they possess it - and they know they bring the King's edict. How marvelous is His love that lifts us from sinful depravity and despair and would lift us above every evil thing and sit us next to the King of Kings as if it were made for us from the beginning. (And so it was!) May our Princehood cause us to act as respected, watched royalty, treat others with the kind understanding of one who sees from the perspective of the High One, and sees our total purpose as fulfilling that place as an ambassador of the King.

# January 8th
## Purging

"For I, saith the Lord, will be unto her a wall of fire round about, and will be the glory in the midst of her."
Zechariah 2:5

Protection without, power within! That fire is God Himself. He shall not allow a single trial or heartache, blessing or desire come to you until it first is perfectly purged, a pure and Holy Thing. And that glory is God Himself, that inner beauty and strength, and an endless reservoir of grace and power.

# January 9<sup>th</sup>
## Conquered

"And therefore will the Lord wait, that he may be gracious unto you, and therefore will he be exalted, that he may have mercy upon you: for the Lord is a God of judgment: blessed are all they that wait for him." Isaiah 30:18

To be conquered by God is a hard, but blessed thing. Like a boy with a sliver, we can't stand the pain but would prefer not to have Father take it out. Those "unconquered" things we grasp so desperately: friends, family or possessions, are those very things God desires to "conquer" so that we need not fear losing anything. That which we grasp, we kill - that which we allow God to conquer opens the door for God to pour out His blessings and peace.

# January 10<sup>th</sup>
# Husband

"And it shall be at that day, saith the Lord, that thou shalt call me Ishi and shalt call me no more Baali." Hosea 2:16

"Baali" in Hebrew means "my master." Ishi means "my husband." In our growth in God, we seem to go through three stages. As young believers, we're so grasped by the love of God that He truly is husband and lover. But then as we develop in our working challenge of marriage with God, we find ourselves responding, "Yes, Lord," wearily, much as a slave would to a master. This is because under His disciplined love, His choices for us sometimes seem hard. We obey out of duty, less from love, though at its root our obedience is a purer act of love than an emotional response. But God's heart longs for us to move on into deeper fellowship where to us comes the understanding that His discipline was not a task master's unreasonable demand, but His desire to serve us, only asking those things that free us from that which consumes, troubles and keeps us from a purer joy, a deeper walk and a more fulfilling love relationship with our Divine Lover, where all our "I have to's" become "I want to's" and all our deepest longings are filled by the One who is Love.

# January 11ᵗʰ
# Cross-Examination

"Examine me, O Lord, and prove me; try my reins and my heart." Psalms 26:2

What a dangerous prayer! No saint of God should pray it without counting the cost. Truly Jeremiah called the heart "deceitfully wicked, incurably sick." Only under the scrutiny and surgery of the Divine Physician can we be cured.

He examines; often we don't even know the prognosis. We just feel the probing, poking and pulling Hand of the Spirit. "Cross-examine me, Lord..." In the divine courtroom, He who is both our Prosecutor and Defense questions our every move, motive and action, until we see the truth. "Test my motives and affections, too..." Even the secret chambers of sin and evil attachments have the Searchlight put on them. When the truth of our heart is out, the beloved Defense Lawyer pronounces us forgiven, while the wise Prosecutor demands death to the sin; we are taken to Calvary; the sin is nailed to His cross, and we walk away free men! Wonderful love of God!

Pray David's prayer only when you are sure it is what you want, for God will answer it speedily.

# January 12<sup>th</sup>
## Concealed Things

"It is the glory of God to conceal a thing; but the honor of Kings is to search out a matter." Proverbs 25:2

Here we have the two divine privileges: God's, which is to hide deeper truth and reserve it for the truly diligent searchers; and ours, which is to pursue those truths and obtain rich joy and treasure in finding them. The treasures deeply buried beneath the treasures of His Word are endless. It is our privilege as Princes and Princesses, Kings and Queens of His royal bloodline, to dig deeply beneath the pages of His Word, and experience the unspeakable joys of His fathomless truth.

# January 13<sup>th</sup>
# Threshing

"Bread corn is bruised; because he will not ever be threshing it, nor break it with the wheel of his cart, nor bruise it with his horsemen." Isaiah 28:28

Have you ever felt guilty because your burdens are seemingly light compared to another's? Have you ever been bitter and angry because your "threshing" seems unfairly measured, a trial much more severe than those around you? But He doesn't thresh all grains the same! Each of us is uniquely special, custom-made by our wise Creator. Your easy burden is tailor-made; God knows the prospering of spirit that comes to you in that way. Your seemingly unbearable load is custom-designed; God knows the steeling of resolve and spirit that comes in that test.

For the light-burdened, don't feel guilt - bless God that He knows how much is yours to bear and has added no other. Yet seek to take even more of His burden, and that of others, for your capacity is great. For the heavy-burdened, thank God that others are not called to the load you bear! God has chosen this because He prepares you for powerful ministry. Envy not the light-burdened. God knows how much each should carry. Remember the old adage: "If all our problems were hung on the line, you would take yours, and I would take mine." The threshing is relative, and what may seem a petty burden to you in another may be a crushing weight to them. Do not feel sorry for those with heavy weights; they are being prepared to rule the stars. "God tailors the trial to meet your need."

# January 14<sup>th</sup>
## Signs

"And thine ears shall hear a word behind thee, saying, This is the way, walk ye in it, when ye turn to the right hand, and when ye turn to the left..' Isaiah 30:21

Mature believers don't need "fleeces" and "signs" at every corner. For those walking (not sitting) in the Spirit, God is faithful to keep you on the right path.

While traveling once, a friend and I had traveled several miles, not sure if we were going the right way. "How do we know if we're still going the right way?" my friend asked. "When in doubt," I quipped, "Just keep going on the last sign you saw." Absence of God's voice is not an indication of being lost: there are often long stretches between the last direction you received and the fresh Word. Until He speaks, trust and follow the last Word He gave - and if you should get off the road, He is faithful to give us the stop signs, dead-ends and detours necessary to keep us on His Highway. Trust that! God has few green lights.

# January 15<sup>th</sup>
## Idols

"I have declared, and have saved, and I have shewed, when there was no strange god among you: therefore ye are my witnesses, saith the Lord, that I am God." Isaiah 43:12

Do you feel powerless? The first check you should make is to see what idols remain in your heart. Does self-ambition drive you? It may be an idol. Do your friends hold you back from the total Christian walk and witness you long to have? They are idols. Is there one person whom you love so dearly that your commitment to Christ wavers? These could be idols. Family, job, possessions, pride, prestige: They can all be "little gods" that keep the flow of God's power from our lives. Let your prayer be, "create in me a clean heart, 0 God," and the Divine Housekeeper will come in that open door and begin sweeping away the idols. Then, His power can enter right behind, bringing new anointing and a deeper love for Christ.

# January 16<sup>th</sup>
# Opposition

"Yea, before the day was I am he; and there is none that can deliver out of my hand: I will work, and who shall let it?" Isaiah 43:13

For the servant of God, obstacles are many. Some are meant to overcome and go through; none are to overcome us, though they seem impassable. The important lesson is realizing when God sets His mind to something, nothing will stop it. We look at our checkbook and say, "God, how will I make it?" But to Him it is nothing, for He has determined to supply our need, and nothing will stop Him. We see the overwhelming work to be done and the shortness of time, and we faint at the impossibility of the task. To you, He would say, "Rest, now, child, come apart for a while; Seek Me first, and you will have the time you need. I am not in a hurry; the stars move as I ordained from everlasting; I do not need you to complete My plan; your labor is your privilege and the seed of your eternal reward. I will do what I determine with no man's aid. Your burden, your bills, your mountain is as nothing to Me. The hills and cattle are Mine. Is anything too hard for Me?" Rest, then - our Sovereign is unmoved by impossibilities, and as sure as He has named each star. He knows your every need and will not delay one single moment to take care of you at the determined, appointed time.

# January 17th
## Dross

"Take away the dross from the silver, and there shall come forth a vessel for the finer." Proverbs 25:4

We aren't instant silver when we first come to Christ. There is often much dross with the silver. Our desire should be to come before Him daily, asking that the dross, some surface and some hidden, be revealed and burned away, that we can be a "vessel fit for every good work." Don't be discouraged if there is much dross, even dross you did not know was there. He is, in His time, purifying you as a vessel to fill with His glory.

# January 18th
## Hidden Treasures

"And I will give thee the treasures of darkness, and hidden riches of secret places, that thou mayest know that I, the Lord, which call thee by thy name, am the God of Israel." Isaiah 45:3

This life is so short. We are taught to pursue earthly wealth, security and possessions. Even some ministers urge us to get our "pie-in-the-sky-by-and-by" right now. But as C.S. Lewis said, "Either there is a pie-in-the-sky-by-and-by, or there is not." And if Jesus' command to "lay up treasures in heaven" is truth, we need to seriously re-evaluate where, and what, our treasures are. His treasures for us are often "hidden in darkness" because they are not in this life. Paul said that we see through a glass, darkly - thus our true reward seems a darkened thing, not to be fully revealed until that day we "see Him face to face."

And what are the dark treasures, the hidden riches? Surely not material things as we know them, for in that place gold itself will be fit only to walk on. They are, rather, the true treasures we all should seek: belonging, honor by God, total creativity, complete fulfillment, the rulership of the stars.

When God turns up the fire of adversity and trial, sorrow or struggle, deep in the furnace of our heart, God is making gold. The coal of our humanity is, through intense heat and pressure, becoming the diamond of our spirit to be worn proudly in His crown. This "hidden treasure," rarely realized in time of suffering, later is shown in our character, attitude, and serenity. While man clamors and strives for things, our God determines to lay up for us treasures that will never pass away.

# January 19<sup>th</sup>
# Answered Prayer

"Thus saith the Lord, In an acceptable time have I heard thee, and in a day of salvation have I helped thee: and I will preserve thee, and give thee for a covenant of the people, to establish the earth, to cause to inherit the desolate heritages;" Isaiah 49:8a

We shouldn't be discouraged when God does not readily answer our prayers. We see only myopically; an infinitesimally small part of an eternal, never-ending plan. When we ask anything according to His Will, (and there's the key), He hears - and we have what we've asked for. Timing is one consideration we often neglect, and we think God is saying "no" when He is only saying "not yet." Circumstances may be right; "common sense" says yes, but if it is not "at a favorable time" then you must wait. Habakkuk understood this, for God had given him a powerful vision: yet God said, "Not yet; but it will happen. Even if it delays, wait for it: it will come to pass." He told him, "write it down," so he could look back and point to the faithfulness of God in hindsight. Have you heard from God, yet no answer comes?

Write it down - wait, pray - at a "favorable time," He will do it!

# January 20<sup>th</sup>
## Counsel

"Thou are wearied in the multitude of Thy counsels."
Isaiah 47:13a

God tells us that "without counsel, plans are thwarted"
and "in the multitude of counsel there is safety." Yet, our
motives are often misguided.

If you have heard from God, counsel is God's aid to help
draw up effective battle plans. But if you haven't heard
from God, stay at His throne until He speaks.

Often when struggling with a decision, I have "made the
rounds" with my "multitude of counsels" only to be
wearied and no more at ease than before. Often they will
say, "You need to seek God," and I must turn back to
where I should have started in the first place.

Seek God, always, first - when He speaks, call your men
of war to confirm, correct, advise. If He has not spoken,
do not weary yourself seeking counsel; your strength an
answer lies in waiting on Him alone.

# January 21<sup>st</sup>
# Unceasing Prayer

"And give him no rest, till he establish, and till he make Jerusalem a praise in the earth." Isaiah 62:7

It is a fallacy that we should pray once, then forget it. Some teach it as being a "lack of faith" if we pray more than once. James says if one wavers in his prayer than it is double-mindedness: that man is not really sure God will answer him at all. "I guess so" prayers and "maybe He won't answer" petitions never get beyond the ceiling of your prayer-closet. But even if you are not sure of the answer, storm heaven for it. The man banging at his friend's door for bread knew he would get an answer if he just stuck to his disturbing petition. God commended him! Knock, Saint, and keep on knocking. Ask, and keep on asking. Not in despair or doubt, but in expectancy. The answer may be yes, no, or wait - but it will come!

"Pray without ceasing." God's intercessors do not rest from prayer, nor let God rest from hearing them.

# January 22nd
# Worship

"I was in the Spirit on the Lord's day, and heard behind me a great voice, as of a trumpet," Revelation 1:10

John's revelation came to him on a day when he was deeply rapt in worship. We seek knowledge and revelation of His word and Kingdom, without realizing that worship is the key. Five minute devotions over morning coffee are good and strengthening, but for those truly seeking a deep and powerful revealing of the Glorious King, they must enter His already present-presence in worship, praise, and adoration, whereby the veil is lifted, our thoughts are captive, and our heart cleared and open to the Voice of His Spirit.

# January 23rd
## Soft Answers

"...a soft answer breaketh the bone." Proverbs 25:15b

God's authority does not require strained vocal cords. "The wrath of man worketh not the righteousness of God." Often we argue loudly attempting to persuade another. The louder we speak, the less confident we really are of our authority in God. It is the soft word that breaks contentious bones. It is the soft words of the child of God who knows Christ as his authority that makes the devils in hell tremble with fear.

# January 24<sup>th</sup>
# Valleys

"And the hand of the LORD was there upon me; and he said unto me, 'Arise, go forth into the plain, and I will there talk with thee. '" Ezekiel 3:22

It is not in the mountain tops that we hear God the clearest. It is while spiritually suspended and seemingly helpless in God's grip. We can't go back, we don't seem to go forward, and all our human and theological devices seem to fail us completely. It is then that He draws us to the Valley of Despair, that He might open for us a door of hope. Like Israel, it is all too easy for us to "forget God in our prosperity." It is when the props are kicked out that we realize how severely we have neglected our First Love.

In that valley, still and empty, is the trysting place for God's beloved, where His words will be driven into our hearts, for the valley has driven us to seek His word. Thank God for those helpless times, these long valleys! They afford to us an opportunity to hear Him that times of prosperity rarely afford.

"Then I arose, and went forth into the plain: and, behold, the glory of the Lord stood there, as the glory which I saw by the river of Chebar…" Isaiah 3:23a

# January 25ᵗʰ
# Not Spared

"Seeing then that I will cut off from thee the righteous and the wicked" Ezekiel 21:4a

Being a child of God does not make us immune from suffering, nor does it guarantee earthly bliss and prosperity. His rain falls on the just and the unjust alike. He doesn't spare us from trials; He matures us through them. The Sword of God that cuts down the evil is the sword that cuts evil out of our cancerous hearts and brings healing. For believer and unbeliever alike, the pain is the same, the suffering the same, and the degree of it is almost indistinguishable. But there is one dynamic, eternal difference: "The ungodly suffer without profit." Or, in reverse, "the godly suffer, but with profit." That is the distinguishing factor that makes the difference between an embittered experience and a growth experience.

"But the God of all grace, who hath called us unto his eternal glory by Christ Jesus, after that ye have suffered awhile, make you perfect, stablish, strengthen, settle you." (I Peter 5:10)

# January 26<sup>th</sup>
## Sensitivity

"As he that taketh away a garment in cold weather, and as vinegar upon soda, so is he that singeth songs to a heavy heart." Proverbs 25:20

Christian, be sensitive! When someone is hurting, it's not our job to "cheer them up" with jokes, smiles, songs and pat answers. Sometimes we're not supposed to have answers - we're just supposed to care. Nothing is as grating when you are depressed than to have some well-meaning person say, "Cheer up. Things could get worse. SMILE, God loves you!" Rather, rejoice with those who rejoice, and weep with those who weep.

Enter into people's pain. Share and feel their sorrows. *We* may be the salt of the earth - but don't rub it in. By truly empathizing, feeling with someone rather than for them, we can be the warm oil of God's love to bring healing and joy.

# January 27th
# Relentless Sword

"That all flesh may know that I the Lord have drawn forth my sword out of his sheath: it shall not return any more." Ezekiel 21:5

For he who has truly decided to serve Christ, God is immovably determined to make that person like Himself, and He will not stop until He is finished. Many are content to just "believe" - they will undoubtedly feel little of the Father's disciplined hand. There is a higher calling; those determined to serve. God has a keen ear for such hearts. Whoever would pray, "Jesus, make me like You, no matter what it costs," will find their prayer swiftly met by the sword of the Almighty Love, cutting, peeling, penetrating and healing. For one who has prayed that most dangerous and challenging of prayers, God will not relent one moment in fulfilling His Holy Work. Are you faced with relentless trials? Search your memory; somewhere in time you prayed "Whatever it takes, do it, Lord." Thank God for it; it greatly delights the Father's heart, that you have given permission for the "thundering velvet hand" to have its way with you!

# January 28th
# Darkness

"The people which sat in darkness saw great light..."
Matthew 4:16a

"Why has this darkness descended?" This seems the most frequent question in times of trouble. But what if all were light? Would we fully appreciate the Light of the World? Would we recognize His presence as keenly? I think not. Just as a candle in the daytime, its light is not the bright illuminator it will be when dusk falls and night comes. Then it will become a great light - a burning path-guide. Those who experience continually untroubled lives never know the value of the light fully. But as one in a dark room that suddenly has the light turned on, it is a great light - dispelling all darkness.

In your times of darkness, you will soon have a great light - you will know "It is the Lord!"

# January 29th
## Fear

"Fear none of those things which thou shall suffer."
Revelation 2:10

Only God knows how much unnecessary anguish is ours because of fearing our sufferings, or fearing that we will suffer. "The thing that I feared has come upon me," Job said. Our fear of a thing is an open door for Satan to pressure and bring destructive forces against us. Experience clearly shows us that the fear of suffering far surpasses in pain the actual suffering. It is a fact that 96% of the things we fear never happen. Nothing is as painful as we imagine it will be, or as permanent. Live in the moment; fear no tomorrow; and avoid premature burial of the good things of your life.

Believe that our God is a good God, and though suffering inevitably comes at times, don't fear it. Even in the suffering, receive God's love and caring arms, and He will turn your mourning to dancing, and you will grow and not fear any evil.

# January 30<sup>th</sup>
## Traps

"Surely in vain is the net spread in the sight of any bird." Proverbs 1:17

Paul's desire for Christians is that they would not be ignorant of Satan's devices. Satan sets many a trap for us. It can be a seemingly harmless relationship that may have seeds of wrong desires, not seen until we are fully ensnared. It may be a slightly underhanded business deal, not realizing the danger until it is exposed and we are trapped in shame and loss of integrity. The Word of God is our tall tree, where we can see clearly any trap Satan would lay. Through the Word, we see the traps and avoid them. We see how even great men of God such as David, Jacob and Peter were ensnared, and we are able to pass by the trap and be safe.

If we continually dwell in the heights of His Word and presence, we won't find ourselves scratching for crumbs on the ground laden with traps of Satan.

# January 31ˢᵗ
# Treasure in the Word

"For the LORD giveth wisdom: out of his mouth cometh knowledge and understanding." Proverbs 2:6b

Only those who have worn out several Bibles have fully experienced this truth. We forget that the Word of God is a Living Book. No joy surpasses the one of reading a verse that has been read dozens of times with no light of understanding and having it suddenly jump off the page, exploding with truth.

Our hearts must be conditioned to begin receiving the "Word behind the Words." This can't be done by quickly reading a few verses before bedtime; we must set aside quality time for the purpose of pondering His Word and absorbing its rich truths. Then, every book, chapter and verse become relevant, exciting, powerful. But you must hunger for it, get alone and quiet before God, asking the great Teacher and Revealer to make His Word alive to your understanding. The reward of treasured truth is well worth the time and discipline of a vital devotional life.

Truly, you will find His Word a living, life-breathing strength.

# February 1<sup>st</sup>
## Sleep

"Upon this I awaked, and beheld; and my sleep was sweet unto me." Jeremiah 31:26

I have made it a habit, not just to seek His sweet communion in the Word in the morning, but before retiring, as well. His Word is the golden clasp that binds the book of each day and the blanket of peace that brings sweet, restful, refreshing, satisfying sleep. And when you sleep filled with the Word, you waken with His thoughts - His perspective - His direction, for "He gives to His beloved even as they sleep."

# February 2<sup>nd</sup>
## Light

"But the path of the just is as a shining light, that shineth more and more unto the perfect day." Proverbs 4:18

What a glorious promise! No matter what the struggle, or how long the road, or how little progress we feel or see, God is doing a work in you that He will not stop until He comes, or we go to be with Him. Often when we feel the most despair, when the way seems the hardest and the struggle the deepest, is when HE is doing His best work, removing inner obstacles, healing inner sicknesses, clearing stony paths so the King of Glory can have a smooth road to travel to our spirit, mind, and emotions.
The more He clears, the more light can pour into us and shine out from us. Like a boarded-up house, no light penetrates. After the Holy Spirit enters to "renovate," light pours into every corner and is a sight for all to appreciate.

This doesn't happen all at once, for it is "more and more," from "faith to faith," "glory to glory." As He is allowed to enter us and prepare His dwelling place, so we are going prepared to dwell forever in His Place, "on the perfect day."

# February 3<sup>rd</sup>
## Surgery

"O thou sword of the Lord, how long will it be ere thou be quiet? put up thyself into thy scabbard, rest, and be still.?" Jeremiah 47:6 (

The answer is, when He has cut out from us every evil thing, every wicked thought, every cancerous sin. For the believer, His sword is a skilled surgeon's knife; double-edged - it cuts going in, but heals coming out, bringing with it all the infections and sicknesses and diseases that keep us from a truly abundant life.

Thank God that He loves us so much that His Sword will not rest again in its scabbard until He has finished His work in us.

# February 4ᵗʰ
## Guarding Affections

"Keep thy heart with all diligence; for out of it are the issues of life.." Proverbs 4:2 3

What are your priorities? If you are not sure, there is a simple way to find out. What are your chief affections? If of even this you are uncertain, then there is another simple key to finding out: 1) examine your time, 2) examine your finances, 3) examine your friendships, 4) examine your thought life. If your time is spent on everything with little given to prayer and devotions, your priorities and affections are misplaced. If your money is spent on lavish things, creature comforts and useless toys, and only a small fraction on God's work, then your priorities and affections are out of order.

If your friendships are more worldly than Christian, if they keep you from precious time that could be spent investing in eternal things, then your priorities and affections need examining.

If your thoughts are obsessed with your job, or finances, or one person, and thoughts of God only come in snatches, you may be teetering precariously on the edge of idol worship.

Whatever you dwell on, you will enthrone; the thing you behold is the thing you become. Who or what is your God? Only a close walk with Jesus will keep your priorities right, and allow His fire to consume the wrong, obsessive desires that influence even our smallest steps and keep us from the fullness of His glory and love.

# February 5<sup>th</sup>
# Added Hours

"The fear of the Lord prolongeth days..." Proverbs 10:27a

How many times we rush around madly, an endless nightmare of things to do! Then you take out your "things to do" list at night, transferring to tomorrow's list today's leftovers. And inevitably, ..there is no time left for God.

In reverencing God, you find time, a definite time, each day to love, praise and worship Him, drawing your strength from His Word, because you know you need it above any other priorities.

Then a miracle happens. The God who is timeless multiplies the hours like loaves and fishes, not only meeting the present day time needs but giving us back the time we gave to Him at the end of the day.

The story is told of two Christian men engaged in conversation on prayer. The one man said, "I'm so busy I can't afford to spend time with God." The other replied, "I'm so busy, I can't afford not to." He understood, as we must, that time with God is the necessary and most important catalyst in producing a truly fruitful day.

# February 6<sup>th</sup>
# Living Hope

"I had fainted, unless I had believed to see the goodness of the Lord in the land of the living." Psalms 27:13

Even with all the promise of heaven, its rewards and rest, none of us are strong enough to live on such assurances alone, and God knows that. God desires, not just that we trust the reality of the life to come, but that we look for His goodness now, in the land of the living. The walk is not all desert; there is always a refreshing stream. Every trial has a termination, and with it, great reward for faithful endurance.

# February 7<sup>th</sup>
## Landmarks

"Remove not the ancient landmark, which thy fathers have set." Proverbs 22:28

It is common for the youngest, newest generation of believers to try to radically change the "old way" of doing things. Thank God for youthful zeal that often challenges our man-made ways. We have much to learn from them. They, too, from us. God has a beautiful lineage in the church, whereby powerful spiritual truths are passed down. There are "landmarks"- set, basic truths that cannot be removed without damage. Tradition, if it is God's truth, is good. One of the reasons so much error has crept into the church is because modern "enlightened" theologians have ignored or ripped up the "ancient landmarks," teaching "new" truth. Truth, if we believe it is God, will always find its roots solidly in Scripture, and surprisingly, taught by our church fathers somewhere in history. I have "discovered" certain truths, (thinking I have a new revelation) only to find it clearly expounded by A. W. Tozer, C.S. Lewis, Amy Carmichael or other spiritual giants of previous years.

It is good to be open to change in our "set ways" - but let's hold fast to the ancient landmarks that God has fathered and so ably passed on to each new generation of believers.

# February 8th
## Enlarging

"Thou has enlarged me when I was in distress." Psalms 4:1b

When we have been under great distresses, we wonder how we can take any more. But God "enlarges" us through the trouble; He extends our capacity to endure. Rather than remove the trials, he raises our "threshold of pain" so we can be strong. And that enlargement is so He can pour into us an even greater portion of His love, that we may comfort many others in similar trouble.

# February 9<sup>th</sup>
# Bearing Witness

"He was not that Light, but was sent to bear witness of that Light." John 1:8

Oftentimes as "people-helpers," we become so involved with the desperation of those we are caring for that we begin to think we are their only hope. Yes, we believe God is ultimately the only help, but still, we begin "fixing" things, over-agonizing and subconsciously believing that if we do not bring healing, the person will be lost. But we are not "the Light." We only bear witness of Him, in word, example, and experience. When we try to be the Light, the person looks to us, and if we fail, it will hurt them deeply. When we just bring the Light, the person will fix his gaze on the Light, not us. And the greatest hope can be given as we "bear witness" - "He did it for me. He will do it for you."

He has not asked you to save the world, but only to be obedient in bearing witness to His marvelous power.

# February 10<sup>th</sup>
## Determination

"Then Jesus turned and saw them following, and said, 'What seek ye?' "John 1:38a

It is not the idle bystander God responds to, but the determined follower. Those who casually wander through their Christian experience, expecting God to do it all for them will never know the inexpressible joy of the God-response. "For He seeketh such to worship Him," who will always be following close at His heels. The devoted, committed and active follower can expect Jesus to often turn and say, "I see you. I hear you. What do you seek from Me?" And to those, blessed prayer answers will follow.

# February 11<sup>th</sup>
## Discipline

"If you have run with the footmen, and they have wearied thee, then how can you contend with horses?" Jeremiah 12:5

Ours is a pilgrimage of spiritual discipline. In order to go from "faith to faith" and "glory to glory," we must also go from "strength to strength," which is not done by expecting God to "do it all for you." We are His "co-laborers" (I Corinthians 3:9). No tennis player ever became famous by just watching his coach play. He may learn by hearing instruction, but he must develop by putting into practice that which he has learned or he becomes lazy, fat and ineffective. Oh, what a spoiled people we are, who consider five minutes in prayer or one chapter of Scripture a pressing burden! Let no one who desires spiritual greatness think for a moment that such a routine will gain them an inch of the Promised Land. "There be giants in the land," the faint-hearted cry, and thus excuse themselves and retreat to the place of safety. Yes, giants are there - and three keep us from being strong conquerors: fear, laziness, and selfishness. Those giants must first be conquered, and if they weary you, how can you even conquer the greater ones? Once in prayer, I was complaining (or excusing myself) to God: "Lord, I don't want to discipline myself in the Word and prayer, I want it to be spontaneous!" "My son," He replied, "You cannot be spontaneous because you lack discipline. First, become disciplined in the Word and prayer, and the spontaneity will come." If you ever wish to truly own the prize of the long-distance runner, do not neglect the value of the daily 50-yard dash.

# February 12<sup>th</sup>
## Inheritance

"He shall choose our inheritance for us..." Psalms 47:4a

Let this verse put to rest the notions that God wants all Christians to be rich, or all to be poor. "He chooses our inheritance." For some, earthly blessing will be God's choice. Others, God's Levites, must rest in knowing that "they shall have no inheritance in their land.. .1 am their inheritance..." (Numbers 18:20). The important matter is that it is His choice, not ours. Some foolishly demand prosperity from God as if it is their right. Others, also foolishly, live in poverty and wear it like a martyr's wound, when it may be due to careless financial stewardship.

God does cause some to be prosperous - those who can be trusted with it, those who will not set their heart on riches, but rather use it for the Kingdom.

God does choose a Spartan life for some - knowing they can better serve Him thus.

Our inheritance is the choice and right of a loving Father who alone knows what we need to serve Him the fullest.

# February 13<sup>th</sup>
## Priorities

"I have set the Lord always before me..." Psalms 16:8a

God's desire for us is that He would be the first priority in all things. He wants to be the deciding factor in even small decisions, the first consideration in every major step. Doing otherwise is trying to build a castle from the sky downward, assuming His foundation will come somewhere at the end. But "except the Lord build the house, they labor in vain that build it." God doesn't want us to include Him in our plans; He wants to include us in His. Our constant prayer should be, "Lord, let me always set You first, before me." Or, as another has so rightly put it, "Lord, don't bless what I'm doing. Let me do what You are blessing."

# February 14th
# Draughts

"For he shall be as a tree planted by the waters, and that spreadeth out her roots by the river, and shall not see when heat cometh, but her leaf shall be green; and shall not be careful in the year of drought, neither shall cease from yielding fruit." Jeremiah 17:8a

To trust God is to have an intimate knowledge of Him, and in that knowledge, neither pressure nor long dry spells cause despair. This verse lets us know that heat and dry spells come regardless of the condition of the tree. It is how the tree is rooted, and where, that matters. Often we worry when long months of spiritual dryness prevail, thinking God has forsaken us, or we are out of His will. But those who know, trust in and rely on God's unfailing love understand that "the rain falls on the just and the unjust," and they are not moved by inevitable times of draught. It is part of the necessary growth process, for every tree planted in God has its summer, its autumn, winter, and spring.

But with our hope deeply rooted in Him, "leaves stay green and it goes right on producing fruit" (Jeremiah 17:8b), all year round. And don't be concerned if no branch grows upward, for it is at that time the roots are growing the deepest into God's soil.

# February 15<sup>th</sup>
## Servants

"Paul, a servant of Jesus Christ, called to be an apostle..." Romans 1: 1a

Notice that Paul didn't say "called to be a servant." Servanthood was not his occupation; it was his identity. Apostleship was what he did, but servanthood was who he was. No matter what our specific call, let us never forget that our identity is as a servant.

"Callings," tasks or ministries may change because they are not who we are. Servanthood never changes; when we are born again, we are born servants. It is in our bloodstream, a thing so high and holy that none should ever think it to be just a thing they are called to do; it is a person they are to be, day in and day out, regardless of occupations, until the very last.

# February 16th
# Divine Help

"I will build them, and not pull them down; and I will plant them, and not pluck them up." Jeremiah 24:6

God spoke this paradoxical word to Jeremiah concerning his people right after He sent them into exile to Babylon. To their human hearts, it must have seemed almost mockery.

Often God exiles our spirit to a foreign place full of loneliness, misunderstanding, and pain. We turn to Him and say, "Why are you hurting me? Why are you pulling me up?" Oh, if we could see His purpose! Our seeming hurting is His divine helping. Our apparent pulling up is His planting. Like little children, our toys must be taken and replaced with tools, our baby-blanket of security, removed to receive a robe of righteousness. It is in that crucible of affliction that our King burns out all the falseness, pettiness and earthly longings. Only in retrospect can we really understand, but even now through faith, we can thank Him for His help and planting.

# February 17<sup>th</sup>
# Mouthpiece

"The Lord sent me to prophesy, ..as for me, behold, I am in your hand..." Jeremiah 26:12a, 14a

The spokesman of God needs no defense, for God's Word needs none. When God gives us a word, hard or comforting, we need not explain it, elaborate on it or defend it. And when we have spoken, we are again as before - just a mouthpiece, an instrument. When a hard word from God has been spoken through us, it is human to want to either run or stand and defend ourselves, for people often, when pricked in their pride, seek to attack the mouthpiece, as the Pharisees did Jesus and the mob did Stephen. This is as useless as an audience attacking a trumpet because its player played a sound they did not like.

It is ours only to speak - and then leave our defense to God. "...and he (Pilate) saith unto Jesus, 'Whence are thou?' But Jesus gave him no answer." John 19:9

# February 18<sup>th</sup>
# Re-Building

"...and the city shall be builded upon her own heap..."
Jeremiah 30:18b

Nothing is useless to God. So often we look at our past - the hurts, mistakes and sins - and can't believe any good can come from it. But God takes our hurts and turns it into compassion for others. He takes our mistakes and gives us wisdom. And He takes our sins, and, when we have been set free, gives us a special key to others caught in the same sins to set them free, with power behind our words because we have been there. Perhaps that is why those who have been forgiven much, love much, for they have seen God do the seemingly impossible in even using our mistakes for His glory. He doesn't waste even the rubble - He builds on it. He turns our scars into stars, and our ruins into mansions. Praise His name!

# February 19<sup>th</sup>
# Revelation

"In the latter days you will understand it." Jeremiah 30:24b

As His last day people, we have the unspeakable joy of seeing all of Scripture fulfilled. God will cause the listening heart and the seeking soul to see previously hidden treasures reserved for That Day, and that people - who would experience the Spirit poured out upon all flesh.

"Go thy way, Daniel: for the words are closed up and sealed till the time of the end." (Daniel 12:9). All truth is contained in, and only in the Scriptures. But not all has unfolded. As we seek Him diligently, we will find an anointing to understand unprecedented in the church's history, in order that He might fully manifest Himself in a people who will see all of man's history reach its end. But we must seek! It will come to those, and only those, who have ears to hear and eyes to see.

"Open thou mine eyes, that I may behold wondrous things out of thy law." Psalms 119:18.

# February 20<sup>th</sup>
## Mysteries

"Call unto Me, and I will answer thee, and shew thee great and mighty things, which thou knowest not."
Jeremiah 33:3

From the Highest Court in the universe comes this invitation that no believer should pass by. He who has created every star and every stone are offering participation in the mysteries of eternity. How sad that so many are content to know what they know and want no more. Here we see the reality of how little we know, for God is asking us to seek Him that He may show us great and mighty things we don't yet fathom. Here also we see the humility of God, willing to share eternal revelations to any lowly human who dares to accept His invitation and seek His face. Before us this day is a choice - be content with our small knowledge and remain ignorant of greater things, or earnestly call out to Him, and experience the daily glory of sharing in the very heart and mind of God, who longs to share them with us.

# February 21<sup>st</sup>
## Adversity

"Thou has known my soul in adversities." Psalms 31:7b

Our trials are the meeting place of God and His child. Our wilderness is the bedroom of the Divine Lover. Although we enjoy God, praise and serve Him in prosperous times, there is something more and more blessed. In that lonely time of testing, trouble and despair, when no one will comfort and it seems there is nowhere to turn, then in the darkness, we begin to behold His beautiful form of light. Here, where all distractions, crutches, forms of escape and earthly comforts are gone. He is finally able to be alone with us and love us without rival. None, but those who have met Him there, can understand the wordless ecstasy of looking into His matchless eyes and hear Him say, "I know you." All the world longs to be understood and known by just one person. Blessed be he who has met adversity and there found that intimate knowledge no human can give.

# February 22nd
## Greatness

"And seekest thou great things for thyself? Seek them not..." Jeremiah 45:4a

We have all fallen prey to the "flesh race" at one time or another. In fact, in our Hollywood-oriented culture, greatness is measured by our popularity, success and physical beauty. Even the church has fallen prey to this, where success is gauged by numbers, results, and talents. God says, "Seek them not!" Greatness to God is not success; it is faithfulness. He is unimpressed with the number of souls "we" saved that we wear like notches in our gun. "For what is highly esteemed among men is abomination to the Lord." (Luke 16:15.) True greatness to God is a gentle spirit, a forgiving heart; patience under pressure, thankfulness in little, faithfulness in a small task. Such things are rarely seen or honored among men, but in heaven, God has laid up great riches and overwhelming honor for such. I have often imagined that heaven's greatest reward will be given some poor woman who scrubbed others' floors all her life, a living witness, loving soul, and uncomplaining saint. God will make her an honored princess! Pity only the self-styled spiritual heroes who have turned their every good deed into a spiritual Academy Award. Truly, they have their reward. Seek only God's greatness.

# February 23<sup>rd</sup>
## Deflected Attention

"...he saith, 'Behold, the Lamb of God!' " And the two disciples heard him speak, and they followed Jesus." John 1:36, 37

This, then, is to be our call. Not to say, "Look at me!" or, "Follow me!" but rather, "Behold the Lamb of God!" And the greatest testimony and praise of God to us is when, upon thus speaking, others turn and follow Jesus.

# February 24<sup>th</sup>
# Truth

"God is a Spirit; and they that worship Him must worship Him in spirit and in truth." John 4:24

Not in spirit only, but in spirit and in truth. How many times have we come to God saying, "Lord, I love you!" when there is bitterness, or anger, or fear toward Him? All our words will avail us nothing, though they are spiritual, unless truth in words and heart come with it. I have often found myself secretly angry at God, yet praying the most eloquent and flowery of prayers. I have since realized the uselessness of such dishonest prayers, and make it a habit to tell my whole heart to God. If I'm angry, I let God know. If I'm bitter, I tell Him why, and if I'm afraid then I confess that fear that I may be free of it. Like the prophet Jeremiah, I have not been afraid to tell God everything in my heart, good or bad, and have found Him not offended, but pleased, for only when I have owned up to my wrong attitudes can He begin to change them.

Deceptive prayers are defensive walls against the voice and working of God. Fear not then, to totally expose yourself to Him; He much prefers your brutal honesty to candy-coated cover-ups of hurtful attitudes.

"For the Father seeks such to worship Him."

# February 25<sup>th</sup>
## His Desires

"Delight thyself also in the Lord; and He shall give thee the desires of thine heart." Psalms 37:4

I can see a little child with Father, laughing, playing, loving, resting, with no care or concern; just to be with Him is enough. This is delighting ourselves in Him! So absorbed, so wrapped up in His tender affection that our only thought is Him!

It is not that He gives us what we desire or crave; it is that as we so delight in Him, then He gives us even our desires; that is, he puts within us His desires that we might be content.

# February 26<sup>th</sup>
# Dependence

"Now we believe, not because of thy saying; for we have heard Him ourselves..." John 4:42a

The goal of every shepherd of God is to teach the sheep to hear God's Voice. If you leave others that legacy, it is a worthy legacy indeed. Perhaps we as leaders fail to do this because we enjoy the dependency others have on us. Like an overprotective, smothering mother, we fear the independence of our children because we lose control, and fear losing their affection. And like that mother, it often has the opposite effect. When our students become overly dependent on us, they eventually resent us because we run out of answers for them. There is a time for all young believers where they believe "because of our saying." But God forbid that we should stop there! Let us lead them on to perfection, teach them to "hear Him for themselves." That way we do not make ourselves the source of their growth; then, instead of resenting our spiritual mothering, they feel freedom and liberty to turn to us for correction, confirmation, and counsel. That vital difference between believing solely because of our word and experience or hearing Him themselves is precisely the difference between believing and receiving the true word and working of God in their lives. Let us diligently endeavor to make that most holy transfer of dependence.

# February 27th
# Consuming Fire

"And the angel of the Lord appeared unto him aflame of fire out of the midst of a bush; and he looked, and behold, the bush burned with fire, and the bush was not consumed." Exodus 3:2

So it is with God's Spirit. Our God is a consuming fire and calls us to enter the fire of His presence. But we need not fear destruction of who we really are, for when we trust His love and allow His fire to envelop us, we shall be as the bush, burning and yet not burned, on fire, but never destroyed.

# February 28th
# The Cost of Wholeness

"Wilt thou be made whole?" John 5:6b

This question penetrates to the very core of our spirit. Do you want to be healed? Don't answer hastily; examine His questioning carefully, for He does not ask for no reason. He asks, "Do you want to be well, not on your terms and conditions and timetable, but as I see fit, in my time, cost what it may?"

Some people hang on to both physical and emotional illness- es because it brings them attention and pity from others. Some cling to their infirmities of body or spirit because they fear the responsibility wholeness might bring them. And others have become so comfortable in their familiar pain that it becomes security for them, and they fear letting go of the familiar into the unknown. Even others tenaciously resist healing because their wounds become excuses for all their human flaws and ungodly attitudes: "I wouldn't behave like this, were I well." But the attitude that cannot change during illness will not be healed, though the body is whole.

Not always, but at times, God challenges us to examine the root of our illness, count the cost of wholeness, and respond to His piercing question that stands as the bridge to healing for us. "Wilt thou be made whole?"

# February 29<sup>th</sup>
## Lover's Response

"When thou saidst, seek ye My face; my heart said unto Thee, Thy face, Lord, will I seek." Psalms 27:8

A heart's call, from Lover to lover. It is a special and precious thing. If it seems a joyful thing to you that One so great as He should long for your love, how much more it should thrill your heart to know that great joy is brought to the Father's heart when you respond to seek Him!

# March 1st
## Only Jesus

"The impotent man answered Him, Sir, I have no man..." John 5:7a

Here we see the other block to total wholeness. Even though Jesus had spoken to the impotent man and asked him if he wanted to be healed, the man only responded that no man would help him be healed. We, too, respond to God that way: He stands with us always, ever ready and longing to heal our deepest wounds, and yet we say, "But Lord, I can't talk to anyone! No one wants to help me! I just wish someone would show me the way to be healed!" How God's great heart must hurt when we continually turn to others for healing when all along He waits for us to come to Him. Man can never do what God alone can. Man is only a vessel. When you cry out for healing, do not weary yourself seeking out others, for "vain is the help of man." Turn to God first, and with all your heart. In His loving hands alone will you find the gift of healing you so desire.

# March 2nd
## Fresh Bread

"Whence shall we buy bread, that these may eat?" John 6:5

When the press of human need surrounds us, we long so much to have more answers, more insights, more to offer. We turn to books, devotionals, and pamphlets we purchase at the local Christian bookstore, hoping that the "bread" we have purchased will provide for the needs. Some of that is good. We find, however, that such second-hand bread, though fresh, seems to have day-old bread staleness. The question asked of Philip was by the Savior taking the present, sacrificed bread and breaking it to feed a multitude. We need not search great distances to find the bread we need; daily, as we offer ourselves to be broken, He will turn His word into fresh bread and use us to feed the multitudes.

# March 3rd
## Kept, Not Sheltered

"I pray not that thou shouldst take them out of the world, but doubt that thou shouldst keep them from the evil." John 17:15

We must be careful that we do not become spiritual isolationists. In this wicked world, it is too easy to want everything to be safe and spiritual. We want our children to grow up in a "moral" atmosphere, without realizing that if the home is Christ-centered, then no secular school can move them, and if the home is unbalanced, even in a Christian school, rebellion will come to light. Christian schools, businesses, concerts, communes – some have a place and importance. But when these things become forms of self-protection, rather than aggressive evangelism, we have done a dangerous thing – we have made to happen about our Lord prayed would not happen – we've taken ourselves out of the world. That is hiding our light under a basket. That is hiding our city on a hill. Not out of but through is God's way – not away from, but in the midst of this world are we to be conquerors. The people who drink, take drugs or engage in sexual promiscuity often do so in order to stop feeling pain – almost a reversion to womb-like sheltering. Let us be careful lest we turned the church into a womb for spiritual embryos. It is not. It is a training center to turn our out mature and fully equipped soldiers to reenter the outside world and bring light to the dark corners of the world.

The church is only the infirmary, the classroom and the launching pad for the larger field outside of it, already perishing for lack of laborers.

# March 4<sup>th</sup>
# Night Instructions

"My reins also instruct me in the night seasons."
Psalms 16:7b

Not only when we are awake does our Teacher teach;
no, even as we sleep the communion between His Spirit
and ours continues. Sometimes it is a dream; sometimes a
strong, indefinable impression we received sometime in the
night. Throughout the day, we are so fraught with earthly
concerns and worries that God fails to penetrate; but in
that most precious sleep time, when our worries are put
aside and our minds at peace, often then our Father visits,
teaches, strengthens, guides. Pray that you would be so
sensitive to His night wooing that even as you sleep, you
continue to receive.

What a lovely thought, to realize that even as we sleep,
we are pressing on! Not even hours of slumber are wasted
in the presence of the Lord. We should not feel, as I once
did, that sleep was wasteful, a hindrance to the work we
could be doing, were we awake. No, in God's provision
even sleep is in the economy of His Kingdom. Were it not
for sleep, Joseph of the Old Testament would have had no
dream, Daniel would have viewed no vision of things to
come, and Joseph of the New Testament would have had
no visitation. In the stillness of sleep, unhindered by
conscious worry, the Holy Spirit may then speak mysteries
to our Spirit. Thank God as you lay your head down, for
"He gives to His beloved, even as they sleep."

# March 5$^{th}$
# Full of Hope

"Blessed be the God and Father of our Lord Jesus Christ, which according to his abundant mercy hath begotten us again unto a lively hope by the resurrection of Jesus Christ from the dead." 1 Peter 1:3

Full of hope...is this not what the world cries for, feebly strives to produce with faint exclamations of "I hope so"? But our hope is not a denial, but an affirmation of reality; not vain grasping at nothing, but solid, confident, joyful knowing that Jesus is alive and we shall live forever.

# March 6<sup>th</sup>
# Fellowship

"For I long to see you, that I may impart unto you some spiritual gift, to the end ye may be established."
Romans 1:11

You have not tasted of true fellowship until this verse becomes your prayer and consuming desire. We have all had the poor substitutes; endless chatter, destructive gossip, Christian parties replete with games and jokes, jesting and excess. How worthless, how meaningless, how empty! All go away feeling they have less than before they came.

Real, life-giving fellowship comes from hearts whose only aim is to see the other built up and richer because of the spiritual gifts they bring. We should pursue this with the heart of a lover longing to penetrate the very depths of the beloved's heart, filling it with eternal treasures and the warmth of caring and love. Anything less than this cheapens the overwhelming gift that true fellowship is. As the hour grows late, let us strive with fervency befitting His last day people to put the eternal building-up of each other as the only fellowship worth our time.

# March 7th
# Hearing

"Why do ye not understand My speech? Even because you cannot hear My Word." John 8:44

On many occasions people have come to me, saying, "I pray and pray and pray, but God never talks to me!" When I ask them if they spend much time pondering and studying Scripture, they usually say "no." No wonder they don't hear the voice of God! For the majority of His speech to us is from His Word. Even when He does speak otherwise, it is always in total harmony with the truth of Scripture. How else can we be kept from deceiving voices, unless His Word is written deeply in our heart like a watchman against the enemy?

If you do not understand God's "speech," it is not because He is not speaking. His Word speaks continuously. We have only to read, that we may "hear."

# March 8<sup>th</sup>
# Debtors

"I am debtor both...to the wise, and the unwise."
Romans 1:14

All in all, I have learned at least as much from those I have not liked as those I have. I have grown immeasurably by those who sought to bring discredit upon me and am thankful for the priceless lessons I've learned by observing those who foolishly waste their spiritual potential. It is in our nature to cut off all people who are inconvenient, unpleasant, cruel or uninteresting. But that is not God's way!

Perhaps we need the patience that will come to us through bearing with an impossible brother. Perhaps through the vicious attack of a gossiping church member, God would teach us greater love and forgiveness. Perhaps through seeing an unwise person ruining his Christian example, we can be moved into self-examination and a strong desire to be kept from that snare. Learn to thank God for every relationship, whether good or hurtful. God give us Joseph's heart, that we may see even those who have injured us and say, "But as for you, you thought evil against me, but God meant it for good."

# March 9th
# Co-Laborers

"For we are laborers together with God..." I
Corinthians 3:9a

Our labor in God is neither all our work or all His. We
are partners, co-laborers with God. He does not expect us
to do all the work, for His power is available even in our
smallest work Neither does He delight in those who sit on
their spiritual posteriors, expecting God to do it all. The
key words here are willingness and cooperation. "Have thy
tools ready; the Lord will find thee work."

# March 10<sup>th</sup>
## Goodness and Severity

"Behold therefore the goodness and the severity of God." Romans 11:22a

We do injustice to the truth and to others if we preach of a one-sided God. He is gentle, caring and a God of blessing. But that is not all! He is severe as well; also stern, determined and holy. To preach a severe God without sharing of His goodness brings condemnation. To tell of His love and gentleness and avoid speaking of His severity breeds spiritual anarchy. At times we see His goodness and blessing; at others, His chastising hand. Let us determine to know them both, and hold the one in remembrance when the other facet seems hidden. And never forget - even His severity is perfect love. The same Jesus whose appearance to John on Patmos caused him to fall on his face in fear is the same Gentle Lamb who touched him and said, "It is I, be not afraid."

# March 11th
## Importance

"For none of us liveth to himself, and no man dieth to himself." Romans 14:7

This is a word to both the proud and the lowly, the self-centered and the fearful. You are needed! Your life counts. You have somewhere to go, something to do, a person to be. If you stay in your own world out of selfishness, you are robbing God of His vessel He intends to use. You are spiritually AWOL. If you hold back because you don't believe you are important enough to matter to God or others, take heart! The race is not to the swift, nor the battle to the strong. God takes even the weakest of saints and uses them mightily. To both the selfish and shy, God has an awesome word for you: the lives you touch or fail to touch, will either prosper or suffer because of your decision. Both decisions have eternal results.

# March 12<sup>th</sup>
## Increase

"...but God gave the increase." I Corinthians 3:7b

In our labors, let us not forget Who it is that brings success. In an age where it is easy to use fund-raising methods and emotionally manipulating sermons, it is easy to attribute growth and prospering to God, when He may have nothing to do with it at all, and we are found with a self-made Kingdom. The true minister of God moves only according to divine, daily instruction. That way, if there is growth, it is known that God has given the increase. And if growth is withheld, rather than wonder why his "methods" have failed, there is instead rest and rejoicing, knowing that God is the author of increase, and if in His wisdom He has chosen a better thing, there is perfect peace.

# March 13<sup>th</sup>
## Irrevocable Call

For the gifts and calling of God are without repentance." Romans 11:29

The greatest mistake we can make is to gauge our spirituality by God's blessing on our ministry. God blesses His calling. His word spoken through us will not be fruitless. He chooses whom He will to do His blessed work. In short, because He does not revoke His call or gifts from a man, then it is entirely possible to be far from God and still see His "blessing" on our ministry. This is a sobering thought. Let us diligently endeavor, therefore, to make strong our personal relationship with God in prayer and the Word, so that we are not weighed in the balance and found wanting. If you are close to God in your heart, then regardless of how your ministry is blessed, you are assured that all is well with you in your Father's house.

# March 14<sup>th</sup>
## Contentment

"But by the grace of God I am what I am." I Corinthians 15:10a

The key to being content in whatever state you are in being content with who and what you are. If you are unhappy and rebel against who God made you and what He has given you, you will never be happy no matter how your circumstances change. Paul learned the happy secret of being content with himself, rejoicing not only in his gifts but also his limitations. The God who knows and loves you so well created you as He saw best. It gives Him great joy when such a one has a thankful and rested heart concerning that creation. Such a one will sing even in prison because he knows who he is, and is glad.

# March 15<sup>th</sup>
# Open Doors

"For a greater door and effectual is opened unto me, and there are many adversaries." I Corinthians 16:9

In this walk from glory to glory and faith to faith, it is a continual ebb and flow of trial, overcoming, test, blessing, pressure, and release. When we pass through a time of testing, it is to enlarge us for a greater and effectual door of ministry. But do not rest in the victory; with the greater door comes greater confrontation with adversaries. But even this is a glory, for God is trusting us to go in and conquer an even greater territory than before. Like good soldiers, we must remember that our Adversary never rests; he surely attacks before victory but is just as likely to attack after, while we are tempted to become stagnant and complacent. Do not fear the greater adversaries - glory in the greater door, and remain in readiness at all times to engage the battle once again.

# March 16<sup>th</sup>
# Off Guard

"But while men slept, his enemy came and sowed tares among the wheat, and went his way." Matthew 13:25

It is when we "sleep," while we are unwary and when we are off-guard that Satan can sow tares in our lives. The position of Christian is always awake, always ready, always watchful an vigilant. If Satan can but lull us into the sleep of spiritual laziness, he will have abundantly fruitful ground in which to sow his unfruitful works of darkness. Much error, many wolves have crept into the church because "men slept." May we always be on the cutting edge of alert watchfulness. "Be sober, be vigilant; for your adversary the devil, as a roaring lion, walketh about, seeking whom he may devour." I Peter 5:8

# March 17<sup>th</sup>
## Secrets of the Heart

"...for He knoweth the secrets of the heart." Psalms 44:21b

Is this not a wonderful comfort? For there are times when even we do not know our own hearts. We are troubled, and don't know why; our reactions, emotions, and desires puzzle us. But He knows every hidden motive, every secret scar and hurt, every buried thing that is in us. He longs for us to turn to Him and allow His searchlight to show us those things that we do not know. For the saint, even the ugly things are shown, not to embarrass us or bring condemnation, but to show how hurtful hidden sins can be, and let Him joyfully and gently consume it by His light and hereby become a little more like Him every day.

# March 18th
# New and Old

"Therefore every scribe which is instructed unto the Kingdom of Heaven is like unto a man which bringeth forth out of his treasure things new and old." Matthew 13:52

God's incredible balance! In the Scriptures and in our experiences, we bring forth multiple treasures to share. The Old Testament would be difficult and incomplete without the New: for only through the New Testament can the Old be understood completely. And the New Testament is fulfilled only because of the foundation of the Old. In the treasure of the Old, we see the golden thread of God's loving plan for man; the New Testament is the Heavenly Garment which the thread produced. The Old explains His character; the New personalizes His love. The old is the shadow, the New, the substance and reality. The Old is the dimly lit picture of man's miserable past; the New is the shining glory of redeemed man's incomprehensible future.

Our daily walk with Him produces the same balance. There are those who only refer to their past, but it is dead unless "He doeth a new thing" every day. And only the foolish seek only new things; they have forgotten the firm foundation on which they are built; they forget their "first love." In His balance, the Old gives wisdom, warning and counsel, thankfulness and foresight; the new things He does keeps our heart young and alive, full of faith and joy.

# March 19<sup>th</sup>
## Bridge of Faith

"And Peter answered Him and said, Lord, if it be thou, bid me to come unto thee on the water, and He said, Come." Matthew 14:28,29a

Many times we think we see Jesus in a plan or a move. He does not chide us for our question: "Lord, is it you?" In fact, it is more than wise to search such a matter out before the Lord. He does not upbraid us for our request: "Lord, if it's you, confirm it; speak the sure word." He is more than pleased to answer, "Come." Then must come the bridge between Word and Fulfillment, the bridge of faith, for He does not say, "Come this way" or "do it thus and so," but merely "come." He will give us no other word of instruction from our boat of safety but that one Word, "Come." It is only as we step out upon that Word that we will find even the most stormy waters as a rock under our feet; if only we but keep our eyes on Him.

# March 20<sup>th</sup>
## Seasons

"And he shall be like a tree planted by the rivers of water, that bringeth forth his fruit in his season..." Psalms 1:3a

The seasons of the Lord! Not always fruit-bearing, for the tree must also have the dying of fall. And the seeming death of winter, when no branch puts forth, nonetheless roots are growing deeper. And thank God, not always winter, for as surely as the snow has fallen, spring holds the glorious evidence of new life blooming once again. The fruit of your growth, the evidence of the deeper roots, will surely be yours again - in His time - in your season!

# March 21ˢᵗ
## Progress

"... .and whatsoever He doeth shall prosper." Psalm 1:3b

The word "prosper" here is full of meaning. One of these is "push forward." I like that. Life in the Spirit is not always full of excitement and miracles, dramatic growth and promise of instant success. God's way is much more sure and secure than sporadic, fleeting events. His promise is that no matter what comes, You Will Push Forward - always advancing, even in retreat - always growing, even through failure. Many inexperienced runners put their best efforts into the first mile and are exhausted in the second, disqualified in the final stretch. It shall not be so with you and I. God's people finish the race by pacing themselves, disregarding the urge to "catch up with the others," for they see the long-distance goal, one attained by steady, paced motion - pushing forward, sure of God's promise of "prospering"!

# March 22<sup>nd</sup>
# Darkness

"He made darkness His secret place..." Psalms 18: 11a

Do not fear the times of darkness and despair. The Lord is waiting for you there! In the lion's dark den, Daniel saw the salvation of the Lord. When the Angel of Death passed through Egypt on that dark night. He protected His own, bringing for them mighty deliverance. In the damp, dark prison, Paul and Silas were visited by the mighty earthquake of Almighty God. Whatever your darkness, God is there in power. "Even the night shall be light about me." Psalms 139:11b

# March 23rd
# Gentleness

"...thy gentleness hath made me great." Psalms 18:35b

Anger only promotes the ungodly. The cruel and merciless may become mighty, but only God can make one eternally great, and He does it by the most humanly incomprehensible means: gentleness. The forgiving Joseph, the weeping Jeremiah, the quiet and faithful Daniel, the compassionate, big-hearted Paul; they are known and loved most for their gentle, caring characters. Our Lord Jesus stands as the most gentle, tender with children, loving with sinners and outcasts; so gentle that even as He angrily cleansed the temple. He yet commanded that the animals be carried out!

Grant us this one virtue, Lord, that we too may be great in Thy sight.

# March 24<sup>th</sup>
# Made to Rest

"He maketh me to lie down in green pastures..." Psalms 23:2a

Unlike God's other creatures, we have little instinct for rest. Our inclination is to run, and do, and work until we are so exhausted that we cannot think clearly. God in His loving mercy will then make us lie down, make us rest, that we may be refreshed. Of our own will, we would undoubtedly not take such repose, but God always has a way to make us do so. He will allow our bodies to become exhausted, that we may be forced to lie down, that we might finally look up. He will remove for a time the things and people that tire and distract, that we may rest in a bed of green that He has prepared.

# March 25<sup>th</sup>
## Divine Teaching

"Him shall He teach in the way that He shall choose."
Psalms 25:12b

In all our teaching and learning, we should remember that it is God who teaches each individually - and teaches according to the uniqueness of our individuality. Principles are good, but God may work one way with this one, another way with the next. The prophets show this; Ezekiel was to lie on his side; Hosea to wed a whore. Habakkuk was to write the vision, Elijah demonstrated truth through dramatic workings of God.

We must be careful not to limit the Holy One in the way He applies His Word. He that searches the heart knows that what worked and was meaningful to me, may not be for you. So let Him teach every one in His way; there are many creative surprises in the individual schooling of our Heavenly Teacher!

# March 26<sup>th</sup>
## Looking Unto Jesus

"Mine eyes are ever toward the Lord; for He shall pluck my feet out of the net." Psalms 25:15

Are you caught in a difficulty, besetting sin or overwhelming grief? Know with certainty that no help can come through keeping your eyes on the net which has trapped you. To focus on that which binds you is like struggling to free oneself from quicksand; the more you struggle, the deeper you sink. Only in diverting our eyes from the circumstances and "looking unto Jesus, the Author and Finisher of our Faith" will assure our rescue. Ours is to stop struggling and look up; His sure promise is to rescue.

"When my heart is overwhelmed, lead me to the rock that is higher than I." Psalms 61:2b

# March 27th
# Book of Words

"...my tongue is the pen of a ready writer." Psalm 45:1b

In the annals of eternity, each of us will have written a book created by our own words. The Scriptures give abundant guidelines and cautions concerning how we use our tongue, that our Eternal Book might be a composition of beauty and love, virtue and praise to God. This thought will cause us to watch our words much more responsibly, speaking blessing and not cursing, help and not hurt, hope and not despair. Through our mouth, God would write an everlasting poem of our lives, filled with peace, joy, triumph, and praise to our God of eternal love.

# March 28<sup>th</sup>
## Unknown Fears

"There were they in great fear, where no fear was..."
Psalms 53:5

I have been pondering fear's great lack of substance. It is empty. It is a vacuum. It is a black hole, a void, with no strength except that which we give it. Alone, fear is powerless, just shadows, noise and show. But alas, when we give place to it, what great a power it then becomes! Then it becomes a devouring monster that gives great fear, where there is no reason to fear. It is a fact that most of the things we fear never happen. Why, then, waste our energy and time while we fear the unknown, unreal, unreasonable. God grant you the grace to expel fear from your heart, for only you can force it to leave.

"Fear knocked. Faith answered. There was no one there."

# March 29<sup>th</sup>
# Overwhelming Love

"Behold, God is mine helper. The Lord is with them that uphold my soul." Psalms 54:4

Have you ever pondered the thought of why kindness has been shown you, why love has been shared when you were alone, why someone reached out to touch you when you hurt? God was with those loving souls. More, God sent them as His love-letter. His valentine to you. Think then of every kind act, every noble deed toward you and every precious friend and loved one and know that it was God Himself with them, loving you with them, caring through them. Who is like Him, who loves us in such an overwhelming way?

# March 30<sup>th</sup>
## Freely

"I will freely sacrifice unto thee; I will praise Thy Name, O Lord; for it is good." Psalms 54:6

What is our sacrifice to God like? Is it grudging? When Go asks of us, do we murmur and complain? If so, the sacrifice, whatever it be, only sorrows His heart. He does not demand. He wants us to freely sacrifice, and with a joyful heart. No father rejoices in a child who does chores angrily, spends time with him grudgingly. If only we would freely and joyfully offer our sacrifices, what tremendous tenderness our Father then know toward us!

# March 31<sup>st</sup>
# At the Center

"My heart is fixed, O God, my heart is fixed: I will sing and give praise." Psalms 57:7

To fix our gaze or attention upon something is to be so centered on it that all else is periphery. In an age when it is accepted that God only has our full attention (if that) one or two days a week, God is seeking those who will never let Him be periphery but always at the center, always priority, a divine obsession. Do not fear that such a thing will produce fanaticism or disable on from fully accomplishing their tasks; if only our center heart is nailed to His, we will find ourselves more creative, more energetic and able to accomplish the smallest tasks with great success, for everything is done for Him, and Him alone.

# April 1ˢᵗ
## Benefits

"Blessed be the Lord, who daily loadeth us with benefits, even the God of our salvation." Psalms 68:19

One of the healthiest exercises of our faith is to make a mental or literal thank you list for all the daily benefits of God. One who tends to complain about what they don't have will especially grow thereby, for if one sets out to know how much there is to be thankful for, he will be quickly reduced to tears at seeing how rich they are. Perhaps if we were to think of even small things, and what life would be like without them, quick perspective would come. The first morning's breath; a bed; clean water; food; health; good friends; freedom; love. How rich we are!

Only those who can thank God for a flower know it to be true.

# April 2<sup>nd</sup>
## Born of Him

"...which things the angels desire to look into." I Peter 1: 12b

God has granted to us, who are only dust, a privilege angels look upon with longing. They are a part of God, but we are His very image! They are created, but we are born of Him; His very flesh and blood. Is this not cause to humbly kiss His mighty feet, wash them with our tears, knowing that we have been destined not as servants but as sons and daughters to inherit and rule the heavens? Angels serve because they were created to. We serve because we have chosen to love Him because He first set His love upon us.

# April 3rd
## Spiritual Sacrifices

"...to offer up spiritual sacrifices, acceptable to God by Jesus Christ." I Peter 2:5b

God does not want your money; He wants your heart. We always think of sacrifice in terms of what we can "afford" to "give up" for God. But if we are bought with a price and are not our own, then the only acceptable sacrifice is everything we have and are. We have greatly twisted the principle of giving by applying Old Testament principles to New Testament realities. The "tenth" is only the starting place. The fully mature one knows that everything belongs to Him.

In the Tabernacle of Moses, there was an altar of sacrifice before the Holy of Holies, before the entrance into the very Presence of Him. The sacrifice was prepared, but the flesh was burned outside the camp; the inner parts on the altar. The "sacrifices" of the flesh, giving up sin, material goods, or wrong ambitions, are only the first steps. The sacrifice that takes you into the Holy of Holies is the yielding of the very desires, dreams and loves of our heart to be completely consumed on His altar.
In that total abandonment, you will find freedom and fulfillment never dreamed possible.

This is the acceptable offering to Him who gave all.

# April 4<sup>th</sup>
## Mercy

"Which in time past were not a people, but are now the people of God: which had not obtained mercy, but now have obtained mercy.." I Peter 2: 10

I remember as a boy laying out under the stars, filled with an awful sense of aloneness. Even then, I had an awareness of being "without mercy." When Christ came to my life, all fear was gone because suddenly the God who made the stars became my Father.

Before, all our prayers fell to the ground in lonely silence. Now we have the surety that every prayer, thought, heartache and fear are intimately cared about, lovingly taken care of. The loneliness of eternity has become the warmth of the caring everlasting arms.

# April 5<sup>th</sup>
## Tested Saints

"Having your conversation honest among the Gentiles: that, whereas they speak against you as evildoers, they may by your good works, which they shall behold, glorify God in the day of visitation." 1 Peter2:12

It is a false notion that we must always be smiling witnesses. I don't believe the world is as much impressed by easy living Christians as we think. They are realistic enough to know that Christians without problems are living in unreality. They are moved not by smiling witnesses as much as suffering witnesses glorifying God. Dead fish always float downstream; it is the salmon, spawning upstream, against the current that is a wonder of strength. We will always be called evil-doers by unbelievers, but it is when the fires are hot and the trials are severe that our true test comes. It is the tested saint that can still smile that causes the unbelievers to know that God is alive!

# April 6<sup>th</sup>
# Hedged In

"My brethren, count it all joy when ye fall into divers temptations; Knowing this, that the trying of your faith worketh patience.." James 1:2

In the book of Hosea, God uses the sorrow of a Prophet heartbroken because of his unfaithful wife to demonstrate His unfailing love even when we are unfaithful to Him. Part of God's plan to "capture" the Unfaithful One is to build a "hedge" about them; inescapable, impenetrable; where all our "lovers" are beyond reach, and we come face to face with our Husband-Creator.

It is natural for us to become so busy with jobs, friends, and even church activities that we forget the longing of our Lord to spend time with us! How it hurts Him to be at the end of our long agenda of appointments and activities. For this, God designs our trials as a "hedge," to get our attention, to separate us from all that would take time away from Him, to show us how helpless we are in our circumstances. That is great cause for rejoicing, for in that place of hedging we can know His special love as in no other.

# April 7th
# Chosen Mercy

"....mercy rejoiceth against judgment..." James 2:13

The unfathomable glory of our faith is mercy. God can do anything He pleases. He could destroy us, leave us, but He has not. He is holy and just and must, therefore, carry out justice. He has every right to punish even the smallest sin. But He has chosen mercy over judgment. Calvary was God's judgment, where every evil thing we ever did was put on Jesus, and He took the sentence of death we would have faced. This is why it pleased God to bruise Him. It was the supreme act of mercy over judgment. And, it is an active, present reality every believer can share. No matter how great the sin, God's mercy is ready to cancel all judgment against us - ours is only to ask.

# April 8<sup>th</sup>
## Tongue of Fire

"And the tongue is a fire..." James 3:6

"It only takes a spark to get a fire going," a modem song says. The tongue has the capacity for three kinds of fire: one is destructive. One rumor, one slip, one cynical or cold comment and we have sparked a deadly fire that my hurt one, or many, and usually boomerang to hurt the speaker as well. Another fire our tongues may unleash is the fire of Moses' bush, the fire of Pentecost - the fire that consumes lives for God, the fire that motivates and challenges to boldly proclaim the Gospel. Through our words, we can encourage, challenge, strengthen and motivate one another to the work of God.

The third fire is a hearth-fire. It warms on a cold night, it is comforting, friendly, soothing. We are also called to bring these fire-words to one another.

The same fire that can destroy a forest can, when contained, warm a home. As with fire, so our tongues. The tongue is neither evil nor good - it is a neutral fire, awaiting use. Let us fully endeavor to use it for comfort, challenge, warmth, and encouragement, lest we spark a blaze we cannot extinguish.

# April 9<sup>th</sup>
## Banquet

"A little that a righteous man hath is better than the riches of many wicked." Psalms 37:16

This is so because the righteous know that all they need is Him. They, unlike the others who lust for more and are never satisfied, fully appreciate and enjoy even the humblest of blessings. They know quantity means nothing. It is the quality seen through thankful eyes that gives every gift the gladness of royal privilege because they have the quality of the great love of the Giver. Such can stand through even the most meager of circumstances; they alone can see a banquet in a piece of bread.

# April 10<sup>th</sup>
## Contradiction?

"For in many things we offend all. If any man offend not in word, the same is a perfect man, and able also to bridle the whole body." James 3:2

"But the tongue no man or woman is able to tame." James 3:8

My love for the Bible grows because of such seeming contradictions. First, James tells us a mature Christian does not stumble in speech; then, he says no one can tame the evil tongue. A desirable goal and an impossible task side by side. Certainly desirable, for the indication is that a tamed tongue brings the entire lower nature under the Lordship of Jesus; certainly impossible for a man, for so says the Word.

Thank God, there is no contradiction. It is impossible for us to tame our tongues; with man it is impossible, but with God all things are possible. With maturity that starts at realizing our helplessness and grows by continual gazing at the Author and Finisher of our faith. He who began His good work will perfect not only a tamed tongue but a perfect God-controlled life in Him.

# April 11<sup>th</sup>
# Growth

"But the more they afflicted them, the more they multiplied and grew." Exodus 1:12b

We need not fear any affliction, natural, physical, emotional or spiritual. It is the way of God that affliction only causes us to grow. Even though Israel's horrible burden seemed unbearable, they were not diminished, but only increased. Only their attitude, as well as ours, kept them from the kind of heart character that would have made it easier to endure the wilderness, easier to find their way through it and find the Promised Land.

# April 12<sup>th</sup>
## Pure Loss

"Yea doubtless, and I count all things but loss for the excellency of the knowledge of Christ Jesus my Lord: for whom I have suffered the loss of all things, and do count them but dung, that I may win Christ." Philippians 3:8

Do we know Him like this? Is Jesus' love so real to us that all other loves are weak by comparison? Do we hunger for Him so much that even our finest dreams compared to Him are as comparing a finger painting to a Michelangelo's David? Paul knew, for in his complete dependency on Jesus, he had come to know Him in a way impossible had he never been broken of his pride in his laurels and status-achievements.

"Pure loss" in the original language can be interpreted in a mathematical sense as "a minus quantity." Paul understood that those things he before gloried in were worth less than nothing because they blinded him to Him who is All. Paul was Paul's ultimate attention. When Jesus was known in Paul's deepest heart, Paul was free from Paul, totally abandoning the goals he once held so precious. In His beauty and love, nothing else mattered, it was less than nothing. That is freedom.

# April 13<sup>th</sup>
## Questionings

"And let the peace of God rule in your hearts..."
Colossians 3:15a

It is in our old nature to continually question, analyze, and resolve things. But for the believer, this is not healthy. The longer I know Him, the more unanswerable questions there seem to be. Rather than taking every outward dilemma or inward struggle to the drawing board, let us stop struggling with useless and empty self-analysis and yield every question to Him who knows all. In that very act, we have opened the way for His peace to settle our troubled minds and hearts and given Him the access to answer, in His way, the questions He knows we need to be answered.

# April 14<sup>th</sup>
## Salt

"Let your speech be always with grace, seasoned with salt, that ye may know how ye ought to answer every man." Colossians 4:6

"The salt of grace"...that which stings a wound is also a healer. That which stings a wound may to another bring out the "full flavor" of truth to others. That which causes a harsh reaction to some will be a "preservation" of spiritual life in the end. Here again, we see the balance of mercy and truth, both incomplete and administers of death without the other. Our words must both cut and heal.

But we must not forget that in order for our speech to be so, it must first become part of us. We must also experience the "salt" that stings our wounds and be healed by them, and be partakers of the truth and grace that has brought fullness of understanding. Then we will know how to answer a fitting answer, for we have lived the very life we will speak to another.

# April 15<sup>th</sup>
## Living Sermons

"So being affectionately desirous of you, we were willing to have imparted unto you, not the gospel of God only, but also our own souls, because ye were dear unto us." 1 Thessalonians 2:8

Words are easy to speak. We hear sermons constantly, read stories, are admonished by every means. Yet, which words do we remember the clearest, treasure as dearest? Is it not from those whose commitment of life to our Lord and others is so total that it makes their words irresistible, penetrating, enduring?

Words of comfort mean little until accompanied by loving arms of comfort. A sermon on enduring suffering is at its most powerful through the lips of a triumphant sufferer who is sharing his death to bring life to others. There is some power in teaching a sermon; there is infinitely more in being one.

# April 16th
# Appointed Trials

"That no man should be moved by these afflictions: for yourselves know that we are appointed thereunto.." 1 Thessalonians 3:3

When trials come, how we wiggle and squirm under their pressure, our one desire to be free from their weight! But "they are our appointed lot." We blame them on Satan, rebuke them. Still, they persist! We blame ourselves, trying to find reasons for the trial. We play our own inflicting Job's comforters, but still, they persist! We blame others, not realizing they are merely God's instruments, and so trials persist. All along, we are unnerved because we have missed the cause. God has appointed the trials, whether He allows Satan, or people, or ourselves to test. We should not fear retreat or defeat in accepting the reality of trials, the inevitability of them, but also the benefit of them. Is not God great enough that if you need to resist Satan, He will show you? Will He not teach you how to handle in a godly way the tests brought through others? Can He not teach you to change that in your life that is displeasing, yet rest and not put yourself under condemnation? Let God be God, and rest in your appointed lot, whatever it may be. For, as Amy Carmichael said in "Toward Jerusalem" not in forgetting lies peace, nor in endeavor, nor aloofness, nor submission, but only in acceptance will we find the peace that brings the benefits of our "appointed lot."

# April 17<sup>th</sup>
## Godly Training

"…but exercise thyself rather unto godliness.." 1 Timothy 4:7b

Godliness is being like God in character and purity. Becoming Christ-like in attitude, behavior, and character is not just a work of God, but a result of being co-laborer with Him. As with an athletic endeavor, we must discipline ourselves to the learning of the endeavor, what we seek to accomplish, what the results will be.

Most important is allowing our Coach to train us. He gives the exercises, encouragements, and corrections. He sets the example for us to follow. He has provided us with the training manual, the Divine Word of God. But all that would be useless if we did not respond to the Trainer. That response is to listen, study, discipline ourselves to follow His commands. He will show us that way to godliness; ours is to obey and to stay close enough to the Coach to emulate His ever-perfect example.

# April 18<sup>th</sup>
## Proven

"I also will not henceforth drive out any from before them of the nations which Joshua left when he died: That through them I may prove Israel, whether they will keep the way of the Lord to walk therein, as their fathers did keep it, or not." Judges 2:20-22

It is so easy to want to serve God when all is well, just the way we want when miracles happen, and life is a joy. But there is no test, no real growth. It's a season when leaves come forth in beauty, but the real fruit-bearing only comes through hard winters when our roots are driven downward to seek His life underneath the barren soil. God often leaves a circumstance, a struggle, a weakness to prove us, to see if we will remain with Him and serve Him regardless of how hard the test is. An untried faith will not stand up to the Enemy's well-practiced assaults and torments.

Learn to stand and say, "Father, if You never remove this hard circumstance, I will still love You." Then when you are proven, He will give you the weapon to drive out the tormentor of your faith.

# April 19ᵗʰ
## Knowing Him

"For I know whom I have believed..." 2 Timothy 1:12

Why did Paul possess such God-confidence? How do we attain such a strong assurance of Him, of our calling? Paul was sure God was able to preserve everything He committed to Him. I believe we have misread this verse to say, "I know what I believe." But it is not Bible knowledge alone that gives us rest and confidence, not theological degrees or studies. Paul had all that, but he had that most important ingredient most people neglect: knowing Him. To know what you believe is important, but to know who you believe is more so. Bible knowledge without intimacy with its Author becomes the letter that kills and ultimately fails to bring the freedom and rest we need. As most Christians do, I went through a time of severe doubt concerning God's word. I knew it was true, yet had no confidence. I read dozens of books on Bible proofs, all for nothing. My place of rest began through the wise words of an elder brother in the faith: "Confidence in God's word only comes through your intimate relationship with Him. As you see Him demonstrate His concern and goodness in your everyday life, your confidence in His word cannot be shaken." How do we know if a man's word is reliable and that he will keep his promises? Only by knowing him personally, seeing that he has demonstrated his trustworthiness to us. Endeavor, then, while never neglecting the study of His Word, to place the intimacy with the Author first in your heart. Then, what you believe will be unshakable, because you know who you believe in, and you will know why.

# April 20<sup>th</sup>
## Patient Endurance

"If we suffer, we shall also reign with him."2 Timothy 2:12a

Jesus learned obedience through the things that He suffered. Shall we learn it any other way? Our King left us an example to follow. To rule well, one must endure well under the most difficult of circumstances. It is that patient endurance of pain that steels the spirit and yet makes tender the heart. A good king must have endured pain so he may judge with compassion among a people in afflictions. We may ask of God recognition, anointing, authority and leadership without being willing to pay the price. The position of Kingship without the pain-tempered character of Kingship would produce a spiritual tyrant - proud, spoiled and dangerous. Pray not, then, to be a king, but that you may allow God to form in you the fire-tested heart of a king.

Only then will you have the strength and maturity to share the Kingship with Jesus who endured all for the Elect's sake.

# April 21$^{st}$
## Never Forsaken

"Let your conversation be without covetousness; and be content with such things as ye have: for he hath said, I will never leave thee, nor forsake thee." Hebrews 13:5

Is this not the greatest of all comforts? Many are the time we let go of His hand, either by thought or action, yet His grace still holds us tight. "Love that will not let me go!"

So often in Scripture words are repeated twice to announce their surety and strength, from the "woe, woe" of the Prophets to the "verily, verily" of Jesus. This is just such a word, one that brings peace and security like no other can. Never, never will He leave us; never, never will He let go of our hand.

# April 22nd
# Walking

"Nevertheless I must walk today and tomorrow, and the day following ..." Luke 13:33a

The "days" of Jesus' life before death and resurrection were walked, even as we must walk. His "third" day when the completion would be accomplished was the goal of the days before, and those preceding days absolutely critical to that completion.

"Nevertheless, I must walk..." God's promise is to perfect that which concerns us. "Nevertheless...! must walk..." In our lives, we know the goal we strive for; conformity to His image. Nevertheless, we must walk out those days of perfecting. Yes, God could snap his fingers and bring us to that "third day," but we would have failed to become what we should. The days of our walking are unbreakably entwined with the goal. The process is as important as the result. Let us not be so concerned with the finish of our course that we neglect the infinite value of each step, no matter how dull, trying or seemingly senseless; in each God-given step, Christ's character of patient endurance becomes larger in us. We know the end is joy everlasting; nevertheless, we must walk, for, in order to reach perfection, every step is part of that work of forming perfection in us.

# April 23rd
# Guidance

"And when He putteth forth His own sheep. He goeth before them..." John 10:4a

Wherever God leads, whatever new venture He calls you into, no matter how foreign, or difficult, or great in scope, be comforted in knowing that your Shepherd goes before you. Not only has He already experienced every range of emotion and test you will face, but He is ever-living and ever-present to clear the path and leave for you sure guidance in every step you are to take. Fear not, little lamb; He loves you too much to make a mistake; He will guide you on that perfect path.

# April 24<sup>th</sup>
## Delays

"Now Jesus loved Martha, and her sister, and Lazarus. When He heard therefore that he was sick. He abode two days still in the someplace where He was." John 11:5, 6

Lazarus died because of Jesus' two-day delay. Had it been us, we would have run straightaway to Lazarus. But because Jesus loved Lazarus and his sisters. He abode; He let him die. I see two very critical things here. First, Jesus was not moved by emotional needs or what appeared to be the "right thing to do." Only God's perfect leading moved the Son of God. Scriptures carry other incidents of Jesus turning from man's ideas in order that He might obey His Father; the wedding at Cana and the advice Peter gave Him not to die are perfect examples. He would have us as well not be moved by circumstances, no matter how pressing. To go when He says go and "abide" when He says waiting is the way to God's glory, and the highest, most loving good for all concerned.

The second is this: often God will not send swift answers to our petitions. He will wait until death has come to our self-will and selfish desires. It is in mercy He "abides." Would the healing of Lazarus been any more significant than Jesus' other works if He had gone right to him? By divine delay, God was glorified, and all the disciples more sure of Jesus' care than ever before.

No matter how painful the delay, God's word to you is sure: "This...is not unto death, but for the glory of God."

# April 25<sup>th</sup>
## Honor

"The hour is come that the Son of Man should be glorified." John 12:23

My footnote reads "honored." What a strange thing, that the cross which Jesus spoke of was the thing of honor! It is so because no one could be trusted but Jesus to suffer the shame of the cross. Men despised Him on the cross; to God, it was an honorable thing. That very act of crucifixion was to God a place of highest trust; it would be to Jesus highest honor; after, followed the seal of that honor, the resurrection.

We often complain of trials we must bear or crosses we must carry; be sure of this, saint; he who has not borne a cross cannot be and is not trusted of God. The greater the cross, the surer you can be of God's trust in your ability to glorify Him in the fire, and you are and will be highly honored before God for enduring. He will place His seal of honor in resurrection on you when the test is done.

# April 26th
## Last Steps

"Now is my soul troubled. And what shall I say? 'Father, save me from this hour?' But for this cause came I unto this hour. 'Father, glorify Thy Name.' John 12:27-28a

Oh, beloved soul, the pressure of your trial is well known by Him! "Now is my soul troubled." But if we are truly to be like Him, do not cry, "God save me from this hour." For this, you were appointed. Whatever your test, know that God has given it for your purification and wholeness. In seeking to be saved from it before its work is done, you are taking second best. The joy of resurrection after the trial is a joy that cannot be explained; you must experience it first-hand. Oh, do not rob yourself of the joy that comes in the morning! Set your face, not to escape, but to endure gloriously. Let your earnest heart's plea not be "let me escape," but "Father, glorify Thyself." As Dag Hammarskjold said, it is the last steps that determine the value of all that has gone before.

# April 27<sup>th</sup>
## Calvary Love

"And I, if I be lifted up from the earth, I will draw all men unto me." John 12:32

It is not Jesus the Risen that holds the heart's affection for the believer. It is Jesus the crucified. It is the point of contact; it is the heart-throb of God's infinite love. The resurrection is our hope; thank God for it! Yet our hearts return to Calvary. It is sheer nobility; it is love eternal. In His cross, we find our refuge, where we are understood, where all our hurts and fears are understood and may be trusted there. In the sheer nakedness of it, we can be naked before Him without fear of harm. Words can never fully explain the compelling attraction of that cross, but those who have been there with Him are never the same again.

No wonder the greatest hymns ever written find their most eloquent utterances at that cross. His nail prints remain forever to remind us of the Cross that cost the God-Man everything. Our hearts wait in joyful, loving, longing anticipation to see Him, who although is the Lion and King, is still the Lamb upon the throne, slain from the foundation of the world. Gentle Jesus, how great is Thy Calvary love. Ever draw us there to You.

# April 28<sup>th</sup>
## Miracles

"Make me to understand the way of thy precepts: so shall I talk of thy wondrous works.." Psalm 119:27

All true workings of God's Spirit are a result of praying saints, sold-out disciples who are willing just to wait, unwilling to launch out in a thing without knowing clearly what the will of the Lord is. Many projects come and go; well-intentioned ventures come to nothing, for they had no foundation which only comes through prayer, which brings direction, which is followed by Power. "Tarry in Jerusalem until the Spirit come." Whatever your Jerusalem, God will bless your faithful waiting with mighty miracles.

He will confirm His word with signs following.

# April 29th
## Hereafter

"What I do thou knowest not now; but thou shall know hereafter." John 13:7

This is a special word for someone today. Circumstances surround you that are frustrating, unexplainable and confusing. Your heart is tempted to fear and despair. Loved ones do not understand, and you cannot explain that which you do not understand yourself.

His ways are beyond yours! Can you accept that and rest in that? It has been too easy for you to think that because He does not explain. He does not care. But how can one explain trigonometry to a baby? He sees as we cannot see. His silence is part of the plan for you right now. If you do not learn to trust in silence, how can you become the servant who has learned patient, enduring trust? In this time of resting and trusting when you do not understand. He is producing within you the very ability to understand, the enlargement of heart to perceive that reason which is perplexity to you just now. "Thou shalt know hereafter."

# April 30<sup>th</sup>
## No Interest

"Hereafter I will not talk much with you: for the prince of this world cometh, and hath nothing in me." John 14:30

My footnote reads "has no interest in Me." There was nothing Satan had invested in Jesus. There was no sin Satan could point to, work with or joy in. God's desire for us is that Satan would have no investment to claim in us, no stronghold or weak area of sin. The Father was greatly pleased that in His Son was a life and light Satan had no interest in and no part of, no thing he could manipulate. His great pleasure with us is when Satan comes to us and walks away downcast because our Fortress is impenetrable.

# May 1<sup>st</sup>
# Pruning

"Every branch that beareth fruit, He purgeth it, that it may bring forth more fruit." John 15:2b

God's divine, eternal interest in us is that we be conformed to the image of His Son. The fruit He desires is not more souls, more ministry, or more church members, but it is more Christ-likeness. And how does He accomplish this? By cutting back. The flesh, if unchecked, produces more flesh and death. When God prunes us, it feels like a death, but tendeth to life only. How can we learn patience without delay and disappointment? How can we learn unshakable joy unless that which can be shaken is shaken from us? And how can we learn Christ's love until we have been touched by rejection and reproach and yet learn to love the very offenders? What often seems retreat to us is the very tool to make us like Him. Rejoice in the pruning. It is not a setback, but a promotion. It is the way to the True Fruit which pleases God, not of works but Christ-likeness. The words will follow naturally.

# May 2nd
# Abiding

"If ye abide in me, and my words abide in you, ye shall ask what ye will, and it shall be done unto you." John 15:7

Here lies the deep understanding of prayer - effective prayer. First, we must abide in Him, remain in His presence. When that is so, many of our foolish and fruitless prayers are left behind us because we know the mind of Him and what He desires. In that presence and abiding with Him, our will becomes conformed to His, and we will have that witness of heart that assures us we are asking for those things that please Him.

Secondly, we need to have His Word abiding in us. If we did not have the knowledge of His will written expressly in His Word, we would pray hurtfully and unwisely. The revelation of His written will is our strongest ally when we go to prayer.

When these two are in agreement, God will move mightily on our behalf.

# May 3$^{rd}$
# Wilderness

"Then was Jesus led up of the Spirit into the wilderness..." Matthew 4:1a

Wildernesses are no new experience for the church. The only new thing is the teaching that wildernesses are from the devil - that trials are not of God. But Jesus was led to the wilderness by the Spirit. In our wilderness, it is the place of proving, dryness, hunger, and confrontation with the Wicked One. Our lives in Christ are like an unmined treasure that is not discovered until the wilderness brings it out. Without the wilderness, God's diamonds would remain useless coal.

If you are in the wilderness, don't fight against it - pray that God will bring out His treasure in you. And take heart - there are no permanent homes in the wilderness for His obedient ones, and the temporary residence will have a joyful conclusion: "And Jesus returned in the power of the Spirit." Luke 4:14

# May 4<sup>th</sup>
# On Guard

"And when the devil had ended all the temptation, he departed from Him for a season." Luke 4:13

Christian, be ever on guard! Satan never rests from his destructive works. He is ever seeking ways to trip us up, and he will never relent.

The original language of this verse indicates Satan's "departure" meant that he had withdrawn an arm's length away, waiting for even the smallest opportunity to ensnare Him.

It is too easy after a great test for us to relax and rejoice in our victory. Do not let your guard down. It is at that time we must be most guarded, knowing Satan is as a roaring lion, stalking any prey weak enough or unwary enough to attack.

# May 5<sup>th</sup>
# Unearned Salvation

"Salvation is of the Lord." Jonah 2:9b

It is within our sinful, prideful nature that we continually seek to revert to some way we can earn or deserve or work for our salvation. How subtle, how devious, how ugly are the ways of the flesh! The minute we do something noble or loving, our heart warms with pleasure and we are sure God will love us more. I have found for myself that even my seemingly most selfless acts are often rooted in selfishness. And I am continually returned to that stark revelation. I thank God that it is so. We desperately need the reminding that "In me, that is, in my flesh no good thing dwelleth." Otherwise, we begin seeking to earn our way into God's favor.

When we are faced with the grim reality of our sinfulness, we either condemn ourselves and hide or seek another place where we are unknown and can disguise the reality and lead others to believe that we are the wonderful loving Christian we really wish to be. Soon our disguise is exposed once more, and it will continue until we choose to face the truth. That truth is: We are incapable of good. We are powerless to change. And we are loved by God even there, and nothing will change that. That frightens us because it threatens our drive to earn our way into God's heart. We cannot; only in our helplessness, our lack of power to change our heart, can we ever allow God to save us from ourselves. When we have had that full glimpse of sinful reality and face it with God, we will know and cry out, "Salvation is of the Lord;" and in our helplessness, we will finally let Him create in us the person we long to be.

# May 6<sup>th</sup>
## Deliverance

"Who delivered us from so great a death, and doth deliver; in whom we trust that He will yet deliver us." 2 Corinthians 1:10

Whether we speak of deliverance from a trial or a sin, we must remember that deliverance is a life process. Some deliverances are delayed, some are immediate, some are history but all are inevitable; deliverance is the heritage of the saints.

"Who delivered us" - past victories to give us present strength and future hope" - "...and doth deliver..." - the present working of the Holy Spirit, Jesus alive, caring, loving, giving perspective to our past, expectation for the now and determination for the tomorrows. "...He will yet deliver us." It is a sure confidence; He delivered me before; I am proof. He is delivering me now; I see His hand on my life. And if that is so, can I not have perfect confidence that He, who is the same yesterday, today and forever, will be my Mighty Deliverer for all my tomorrows?

# May 7<sup>th</sup>
## Sanctification

"Cease to do evil; learn to do well." Isaiah 1:16b, 17a

This Old Testament word sums up the New Testament principle of sanctification. I would not dare suggest it is something we can do in our own strength. But it does lay down a simple insight into God's working His Holiness into us. God empowers us to cease evil-doing. You do not *learn* to stop doing evil; it takes a divine deliverance for us to cease from sin. And we do not just *start* doing good. We must learn how by letting Him show us what is good. Sinful action is not so much learned, as it is an automatic response to our evil nature. But doing *good* is *not* automatic, but must be taught to us by Him who knows no evil but is only good.

# May 8<sup>th</sup>
# His Work

"Lord, thou wilt ordain peace for us; for thou also hast wrought all our works in us." Isaiah 26:12

After all is done, and we lay our earthly tabernacle down and stand before Him, no matter how much we have done for the Name of Christ, it is still He who has been the start, and completion of it all. He has wrought all our works in us. He gives the desire to serve Him; He equips. He sustains, and He finishes. It is He who began the good work in us who shall perform it. The Scriptures remind us that there is nothing we have that we have not been given. This is humbling, but it is rest. We are only responsible for obeying the voice of God. The resources are there. Every worker in the Kingdom needs to realize this. Then, if there is success, there is no pride, and if it results in failure in our human eyes, we are not defeated for He is sovereign and works even in seeming failure. Our ordained peace comes only when we know we can rest, not in our work, nor be distraught at hindrances, but to release it all to Him who is the First, Last, and everything in between.

# May 9<sup>th</sup>
## Lordship

"O Lord, our Lord, other lords beside thee have had dominion over us: but by thee only will we make mention of Thy Name." Isaiah 26:13

Our reference point is not what we were, but who He is. Our testimony should not focus on our past sins, but on who we are becoming because of Him. Too many testimonies gain their impact form how sinful they were. Many of those testimonies fall by the wayside because the attention past sins are given continues to make those sins lords. What we were is forgotten by God. Only who we are, and what we will become will remain.

Other lords have had dominion, but His name is the strength of freedom and our center of present attention.

# May 10<sup>th</sup>
## From Milk to Meat

"Whom shall He teach knowledge? And whom shall He make to understand doctrine? Them that are weaned from the milk, and drawn from the breast." Isaiah 28:9

The transference from milk to meat is a vital one. You can only feed a baby milk for a time. If it is prolonged past that time, severe depletion will take place, sickness, and eventual death. Strong meat makes healthy children and fit adults. In the process of God, it is good and right that we are taught at the hand of others; that is milk. But that process must wean us to meat; that which God alone teaches and we eat daily from His Word. That does not mean we do not learn from others. I often eat at others' tables, knowing they have prepared it. Yet, I must feed myself still, though meat is placed before me. The need of this hour is for believers to stop being satisfied with the bottle-feeding that leaves us free of action and responsibility. Those who desire true knowledge and understanding must let God wean them from spiritual dependency and let Him be the Teacher. One need not fear error, for there is no more stern and determined teacher than He. I fear more for them who depend on a man, for if he should err, they will follow blindly. We must share recipes, but we are not wise to let another do all our meal-preparing for us.

# May 11<sup>th</sup>
# Plans

"I have declared my ways, and thou heardest me: teach me thy statutes." Psalm 119:26

Don't just tell God what you are going to do. Tell Him, then wait for His answer, confirmation, and direction. Many a plan is thwarted because we simply tell God our intentions, then expect Him to bless it. In our human wisdom, we cannot make even a vision from God come to pass. This is God's way: we tell Him the what of our plans, and as we wait on Him, He will tell us the how, the when and the where. To fail to perceive this is to end plans before they have even begun.

# May 12th
## Confusion

"And some cried one thing, some another, among the multitude: and when he could not know the certainty for the tumult, he commanded him to be carried into the castle.." Acts 21:34

We know that Satan is Lord of confusion, but how do we deal with it? It is often not enough to rebuke him, because the reason he can confuse us so readily is that the intermediate agency of our mind is so vulnerable. We must take steps, in times of confusion, to take authority over our own minds, giving no place to the devil at all.

It is my belief that in a time of confusion and decision, it is of utmost importance that we do not panic. Fear creates confusion. Fear is a lack of trust that God will answer. The more we sit and worry, casting in our minds this option and that disadvantage, the more we block Him from reaching us at all. It is like a glass jar filled with soil and water. Shaking the glass will only cloud the picture. If you just let it sit, it will soon settle, and you can begin to see clear layers, patterns, and settings. This is why we must calm our hearts, change our focus and put away the thousand "what ifs" that come in times of questioning. Do not fear God will neglect your need for and answer if you fail to attend to it. And do not forget that being consumed by the decision will bring fear to numb your heart to His speaking. Answers do not come from debating the questions: they come from knowing God is our source. Put all questionings aside, then; dwell in His presence; His answer will come.

# May 13<sup>th</sup>
# Purposed

"But Daniel purposed in his heart that he would not defile himself..." Daniel 1:8a

We must have God's grace to overcome besetting sins; striving against sin in our flesh is only futile and leads to guilt and legalism. Where we have erred in obtaining grace is from the other perspective: we will give up sins when God gives us grace and takes away our desire to sin. This also is an error, leading to failure. The key is what we purpose in our heart. We may outwardly ask God to help us overcome sins, inwardly being quite unwilling to give them up. God cannot help us then. But what is at the center? Are you purposed not to defile yourself, or are you secretly loving your sin while outwardly proclaiming your desire to be free? Perhaps that is so; even then, if you are willing to confess that, God may still work. "Lord, I don't want to stop. Please put the desire in me!" In your honesty, God may then begin to put His desire for holiness into you. He will give you the strength that will put in you the determinaion to not defile yourself.

# May 14<sup>th</sup>
## Eternal View

"While we look not at the things which are seen, but the things which are not seen; for the things which are seen are temporal; but the things which are not seen are eternal." 2 Corinthians 4:18

In all circumstances, take the eternal view. All earthly things will pass; only the eternal remains. Learn to discern between the permanent fixtures and the temporary props. Let your prayer in time of suffering be, not "How can I get out of this?" or "How can I change things?", but rather, "Father, what eternal truth do you want to teach me through this? How can I distill the everlasting elixir from this? Help me to see the eternal reality in the midst of this temporary trial."

# May 15<sup>th</sup>
## Imitation Love

"Let love be without dissimulation. (Hyporcisy) Abhor that which is evil; cleave to that which is good.." Romans 12:9

It is far too easy to speak of love in general terms. Often ours is a Peanuts' philosophy: "I love humanity. It's people I can't stand." God put a high priority on honesty in relationships. That is why the Scriptures give clear guides to resolving conflicts, that we may love.

The only thing that sets us apart from any other social clique is genuine love. Imitation love (which we are far too often guilty of) pats on the back and says, "be warmed, be filled." It is in word only. And what good is telling a brother you love him if you tear him down before another? Imitation love is a noun only. Genuine love is a verb and an action word. We seem to have no problem with the passage concerning laying down our lives for one another, having placed it in terms of being run over by a car while we attempt to spare another. But I think our understanding is limited. Genuine love does not speak of laying down our lives in some noble, ambiguous (and thus distant and without requirement) future scenario, but today, here and now, laying down our lives for each other - under fire of misunderstanding, in toils of spirit, in frustration of purpose - regardless of personal cost. Genuine love is single-minded consideration of the others' best - cost us what it may. "My little children, let us not love in word or in tongue, but in deed and in truth." 1 John 3:18

# May 16<sup>th</sup>
# Momentum

"Rejoicing in hope; patient in tribulation; continuing instant in prayer." Romans 12:12

We shun the disciplines of the Spirit. Our society has placed a high premium on spontaneity in things and relationships. The exacted price of this premium has been the shunning of anything requiring work, effort or difficulty. So it is with prayer. It is the last thing on our agenda. It is a task of desperate moments rather than continuous communion. But prayer is a spiritual discipline requiring our attention and time. It does not develop naturally.

Satan hinders it because it is a threat. Our flesh whimpers at its rigor because the feeding of our spirit requires death to our flesh. Prayer begins with an attitude, a determination to be mindful of God's presence. Then one must determine to set aside time every day for communion in prayer and the Word of God. Do not concern yourself with taking hours at first; take a few minutes or an hour; little with God is much; He will multiply it. Prayer begins to gain momentum until the discipline becomes a pleasure, then a need, a necessity. God's people cannot afford to be without this discipline. It will not be gained without a battle, but the momentum gained through daily discipline will lead to a powerful, fulfilled walk in the Spirit.

# May 17th
# Atonement

"In mercy and truth atonement is provided for iniquity." Proverbs 16:6a

When we sin, we can make two mistakes. One is to accept God's mercy and forgiveness without facing the deadly reality of sin. This leads to a continuing pattern of sinning without change. The other mistake is to face the truth of our sin without receiving God's mercy. That causes us to lose heart, live in failure, defeat, and condemnation. Thank God that His provision for sin brings us into complete restoration; truth to change us, and mercy to heal us. By accepting both, we can come boldly without condemnation or presumption, and receive power to overcome.

# May 18th
## Rest

"Thou compassest my path and my lying down, and art acquainted with all my ways. " Psalms 139:3

We are creatures of busy-ness. We rarely have the common sense to rest when we should, if at all. Some of us even keep busy in our sleep, rehearsing the day and anticipating tomorrow. I have found ministry to be a way of perpetuating my own workaholism. "But God's work never stops." That's right; His doesn't, but ours should.

Even a cursory reading of the Gospels will give abundant evidence of the value of rest, for our Lord Jesus frequently retreated from the people to rest, pray and fellowship with those closest to Him. If so for Him, how much more for us! Ministry is pouring out. We must be poured back into.

In ourselves, we do not know when we need retreat, and often continue furiously long after crossing the exhaustion line. Listen, then, carefully for His still voice that knows the path ahead, and knows exactly when you need rest. Obey that call to rest, that you may return refreshed to your daily tasks.

# May 19th
## Holy Addiction

"...and that they have addicted themselves to the ministry of the saints." 1 Corinthians 16:15b

How I long for such an attitude! Not just that serving our brothers and sisters would be second-nature, but that it would become a holy addiction. God's desire is not that service would become a burden. And it goes far beyond a simple desire to serve; it should become a consuming desire, even as with our Lord as He walked among us. May God bring us to the place where we are discontent unless we can continually be about our Father's business, seeking out with fervent love our place of service and our people to serve.

# May 20th
# Thorns

"For thus saith the Lord to the men of Judah and Jerusalem, Break up your fallow ground, and sow not among thorns.." Jeremiah 4:3

When we lose our first love for Jesus, two things happen: first, our hearts become hard; then, thorns begin to grow. While the hardness dries up the good ground, the thorns begin to choke the good growth.

I have found three necessary elements for plant growth in my garden: proper watering, breaking up the hard ground around the young plants, and constantly pulling weeds. In the same way, we must let His "living water" in prayer and study drench our parched hearts. Then, we must be broken before Him, broken in love for Him. And, finally, we must pull the weeds of waste, sin and worldly care from our minds and hearts. Jesus said to the church which had lost its first love, "Do the first works."

Rekindle the plowing, nurturing, purging love for God in your life. The Divine Gardener will do the rest, and no good seed will perish.

# May 21ˢᵗ
## Veils

"Nevertheless when it shall turn to the Lord, the veil shall be taken away." 2 Corinthians 3:16

Jeremiah declared that the heart of man is deceitfully wicked. We are born in deceit, and live a lie until we come to Christ. Even after we come to Him, there is much work to be done in unraveling the self-deceptions. We are often in confusion because our flesh rebels at His Lordship. Things become unclear, problems abound. This is His way. He allows it so that we may become helpless to unravel the lies and confusion, turn to Him and, as we singly behold Him, He lifts veil after veil and sets us free. He delivers us from our pride and pretenses a little more each time we turn to Him in our need and makes room for more of His glory to shine from us, unhindered by the veil of the flesh.

# May 22<sup>nd</sup>
## Terror

"Be not afraid of sudden fear..." Proverbs 3:25a

It seems to be in our nature to always think the worst. I have had several bouts of "sudden terror" - all of which came to nothing. It is a sense of impending disaster; a loved one not coming home on time; a distressing report yet unconfirmed. Suddenly, fear, panic-fear, seizes us, and we can think of nothing else.

My mother gleaned a bit of wisdom along her way which has helped me: when you hear horse hooves, don't think "zebra." It's probably just a horse. In other words, don't blow a matter out of perspective through fear of the worst. We, as Christians, should best know that fear is not of God. We must arm ourselves with the knowledge that fear cuts us off from receiving God's love. It has helped me in times of "sudden terror" to remember that statistically, the overwhelming majority of fears we have, never come to pass! Also, I remember that wonderful comfort of Romans 8:28, that God is at work in all things to produce Good; therefore, I need not fear even fearful events. God is with us. There are no accidents for God's child. And, I can reject fear of even the fearful because of His love and care for me.

# May 23<sup>rd</sup>
## Life Through Death

"So then death worketh in us, but life in you." 2
Corinthians 4:12

Do not despair when you are passing through a time of
suffering which seems like a death. There is a holy purpose
in it. Through it, you can turn and minister life to those
enduring the same trial. The most comforting words I have
received in a time of trial have been through those battle-
scarred saints who have put their gentle hands on my
shoulder and said, "I know, I've been there." They are living
sermons, flesh-and-blood testimonies to the faithful love
of God. Through their death, they have given to me life,
and hope, and strength to stand my test.

# May 24<sup>th</sup>
# Without a Message

"I have not sent these prophets, yet they ran. I have not spoken to them, yet they prophesied." Jeremiah 23:21

Two things can be noted here which are very relevant to our present conditions. First, ours is a fast-paced, reckless, performance-oriented age. "Doing something for God" is pressed as a high priority. If we have no vision, we invent one built on self-promotion and busy-work. Few wait upon the Lord's Word and direction. So much is expected of us that if we stopped everything until we heard from God, we would be considered foolish and unproductive by others - and we fear that. Yet if we do not seek that divine Word, we become like a messenger boy without a message - a delivery boy without a package. It is better to be in God's presence waiting, though the waiting be long, than to run off without anointing, blessing or any spiritual value.

The second thing to note is that those without a message run - but those with true call and anointing can walk with the calm grace of Jesus, who although He had an urgent message and a short time, still had time to be with His Father. It was, indeed, that time that gave Him the quietness of Spirit and strength of resolve to carry out His purpose, even to the death of the cross.

# May 25<sup>th</sup>
## After-Attack

"But after they had rest, they again did evil before Thee." Nehemiah 9:28

It is not trial and adversity we should fear, but the time after victory has been wrought. No child of God should rest on their laurels. We are called as soldiers, granted reprieve but never discharged from the war. It is a principle of the Spirit that if Satan does not win by attacking just preceding a great victory, he will wait until we are reposed by heady success and attack with full force. Enjoy your rest and your victory, Saint - but never take your hand off your sword.

# May 26<sup>th</sup>
## Near

"Am I a God near at hand, and not a God afar off?"
Jeremiah 23:23

Our concept of God being "up there, somewhere" can greatly hinder our walk with Him. It is, indeed, a walk with Him, for He never leaves our side. We cry out, "God, where are you?" and He is nearer than our own heartbeat. To ask God to be with us throughout the day is to not understand that for Him to be otherwise is an impossibility. The God who created the stars humbled Himself as a man so He could live in us, promising to never leave us. Is that not a great comfort? Because of this awesome reality, we can have great boldness, knowing that we do nothing "without the Father." May this also bring great conviction, knowing that even when we sin, God is present, watching, hurting in the destruction of our sin.

# May 27<sup>th</sup>
# Redemption

"He hath delivered my soul in peace from the battle that was against me: for there were many with me.." Psalm 55:18

Most of us have been through trials and circumstances that seem to threaten our very sanity. We believe we will survive, but we fear that we may have to survive in several pieces instead of one!

But this rock from scripture is a balm for the troubled and tested saint. He will not only redeem you, beloved of God: He will redeem you in *peace!* We fear that pieces of our mind and heart are being ravaged in the battle's heat and that we will never regain lost ground. Dear friend, if you only knew! No saint who looks to Jesus in dark times needs to fear destruction. Not only will you come out not harmed, but you will have more peace and power than you could have ever gained if you had not walked through the fire.

# May 28<sup>th</sup>
# Keepers

"Am I my brother's keeper?" Genesis 4:9

Finding the balance to this question is an ongoing quest. Yes, we are responsible for another in ways we often fail to realize. A new face comes to church: Are we concerned enough to go beyond obligatory conversation? Do we remember their name? Are we caring enough to make time to get to know them outside the four walls? And what if that person hasn't been at church for several weeks? Will we pursue them? Are we concerned about their spiritual welfare? We must remember that the Prophet's condemnation came on the shepherds who did not go after the stray sheep. Yes, we are our brother's keeper in many ways. And in other ways, we are not. Every person stands or falls on their own personal relationship with the Chief Shepherd. While we should always be concerned and available for one another, we can't cripple one another with indulging love, or overprotecting sympathy.

I have found valuable understanding in verses that once appeared to be a contradiction to me: "Bear one another's burdens and so fulfill the law of Christ." (Gal. 6:2) "For every man shall bear his own burdens." This seeming contradiction becomes our understanding balance when we understand the original meaning: The first refers to that burden which is unbearable alone. The second refers to a soldier's pack. That backpack we should bear alone as our needed burden for growth and developing strength. We are our brother's keeper - but not his backpack bearer. May God give us discernment to know the difference.

# May 29th
# Ishmael

"And Abraham said to God, "Oh, that Ishmael might live before You." Genesis 17:18

God has taught me many important lessons through Ishmael. One of them concerns the flesh we daily deal with. God speaks promise to us. Then, in our anxiousness, we seek to fulfill that promise ourselves. Moses struck the rock in an act of anger. Peter resisted Jesus' path to Calvary because he wanted a Savior from fleshly bondage, not true spiritual deliverance. Moses, again, heard God's call to deliver His people - but killed a man in his own anger. And, of course, Abraham, who tried to "help God" by producing a "son in the flesh." Is it not so with us? We want the promise without patience, problems, and pain. We rush ahead and "produce" a fulfillment, later to find it was of our own making and built on sand. Then, in God's mercy, He begins to tear down the self-edifice, and we cry like Abraham, "Oh, let it live!" The flesh is ever whimpering, a proud and stubborn obstacle. It hurts to admit we missed God, or built a thing out of ego, or pushed forward in human anger. But God would be unkind to let us continue with our sand castle, for the taller it becomes, the harder it falls. If you find yourself in this place, allow our loving Father to tear down every self-advancement and take away every son of the flesh. He will surely fulfill His good word to you; only this, that you would put no Ishmael before His coming Isaac.

# May 30<sup>th</sup>
## Seek

"Seek Your servant..." Psalm 119:176

All the preaching on standing on God's Word is commendable and right. But as with anything, often our weak hearts are overcome. Often in a weary wilderness, we need the reassurance of God's care. Sometimes we despair as Elijah and sit down to die. We know, in our minds, of God's care. We know, in our minds, we are not forgotten or alone. But our hearts are longing to be filled with tangible evidence of God's care. Like a little child running away from home, we put our belongings in a bandana and go hide under the porch, hoping, praying that our presence is missed, that someone will notice our absence. We are like that with God. "I just want to know that if I walk off or go astray, You will notice!" How wonderful to know that He who knows our tiniest thoughts is always watchful. He cares not just for the one lost sheep, but the lost coin in the house as well!

There are times we need more than mental assent to God's love: We need Him to seek us in our deepest need, to prove Himself in our hour of doubt. He is faithful to do so, and will not chide the hurting soul that now asks.

# May 31ˢᵗ
## Instruction

"Thou that sayest a man should not commit adultery, dost thou commit adultery? thou that abhorrest idols, dost thou commit sacrilege??" Romans 2:22

"Knowledge puffeth up," Paul told the carnal Corinthians. Our greatest danger still remains "preaching what we do not practice." It is so much easier to instruct others in the "right ways of the Lord" than to walk in them ourselves. It is easier to see the faults in others than to face ourselves in our own depravity. When people look to us, it gives us a sense of pride and fulfillment, but it should only create in us a sense of responsibility and a desire to be before God to learn how to walk out truth before we teach it.

# June 1<sup>st</sup>
## Acceptance

"Shall we indeed accept good from God, and shall we not accept adversity?" Job 2:10

It is the cry of every human heart to be accepted just as it is - just for who we are. This is a God-instilled longing, for the God who has made us in His image and likeness has that same desire in His heart. So often we are like fair-weather friends to God; when He blesses us, we bless Him. We keep a record of the positive, joyful and uplifting verses. All that is good! But too often we ignore the verses that are uncomfortable or not to our liking, and when some adversity comes, we are angry, sulking, pouting children, wondering if God loves us at all. How that must hurt Him since He has designed even adversities as a good thing whose result is glorious and joyful.

We cannot accept what we like about God and discard the rest. He longs that we would accept Him just as He is, for everything He does or allows, trusting always, even though we may not understand the reason for sent trials: let us embrace it all, bitter or sweet, knowing the end of all things will be pleasures at His right hand forevermore.

# June 2nd
## Testimony

"He (John) was not the Light, but he existed that he might give testimony concerning the Light." John 1:9

God grant that we might know our reason for existence is to give testimony concerning the light! We are not the light - we only reflect the light. In our words, actions and character we must reflect the Living Christ. His light is forever imprinted in our spirit. We need only, and more each day, simply release that light, Jesus Himself, to shine more and more through every portion of our being. As ambassadors to the Throne, He desires us to represent Him not only in words but in character and display of obvious citizenship differences. That is why we exist - that we may too be part of the whole earth that manifests the glory and reality of our Supreme Lord.

# June 3rd
## False Comfort

"For they had made an appointment together to come and mourn with him." Job 2:11

For all their good intentions. Job's friends, in the end, did exactly the opposite of what they had set out to do. They came to comfort; they cruelly condemned. They intended to mourn; they unknowingly mocked. Like many of us, we are too full of questions in a time of another's tragedy, so we "invent" answers.

Most of us know a situation like this: someone goes to comfort a mother who lost a child, and they say, "Read Romans 8:28. Trust God!" Or, the man in the hospital whose visitors ask why he didn't have faith for healing, or worse yet, what sin caused this punishment from God?

Beloved, good intentions are never sufficient. The deeper the tragedy, the more we must have the wisdom, kindness and godly love to comfort those in need. And remember, it is very often better to be kind than to be right.

# June 4<sup>th</sup>
## Centered

"To whom God would make known what is the riches of the glory of this mystery among the Gentiles; which is Christ in you, the hope of glory..." Colossians 1:27

Christ is the Gospel - the good news! The first, the last, and the center of it all. The desire of the Spirit is to keep us continually at that center, in Christ, and with Christ. It is not in programs or causes. It is not in works nor morals. It is only in relationship to Him who died and rose for us.

To stay in that center is a daily task. Everything, it seems seeks to take our attention away from the heart of it all. This is why church becomes a social, and a true mission becomes a program.

We have left the center - Christ Himself. Examine yourself daily in this. Let the day begin centered in your relationship with Christ. Let every necessary task be done unto Christ, for and with Christ; and avoid all activity not centered in His love and purpose for you.

# June 5<sup>th</sup>
## Silence

"So they sat down with him on the ground seven days and seven nights, and no one spoke a word to him, for they saw that his grief was very great." Job 2:13

As with many verses in the Bible, two lessons can be learned from one incident. It may at first seem to be two mutually exclusive lessons in the actual event, but the lessons are valuable regardless of the intentions of those involved in the story. The first lesson from this verse is that there is wisdom in silence. When we are quick to invade someone's grief with human wisdom and pat answers, God often would have us just remain quiet. Sometimes "I don't know" is better than answers given in panic. If Job's friends had simply done that, they would be commended at this point. But they did not! The second lesson here is that Job's friends didn't go far enough. Though silent for lack of answers, that should not have kept them from expressing care and concern other than their actual presence. In times of grief, someone just saying, "I don't understand, but I love you, and I'm here," can say more than volumes of words. I have to wonder if Job's friends' silence does not indicate fear: they had not known God to allow such a tragedy. Perhaps they were afraid it might happen to them as well. Such silent fear is a message in itself. From that silent fear comes the flurry of words that is only an attempt to quell our own confusion.

In expressing open love to a grieving heart, we cannot only provide great comfort but silence our own fears.

# June 6<sup>th</sup>
## Expectancy

"My soul fainteth for thy salvation: but I hope in thy word.." Psalm 119:81

A father was watching his son make preparations to go off to school in another city. The son had incurred a large debt as well and planned on working to pay it back. The father, realizing his need to let the son make his own way, nevertheless cautiously offered, "Son, would it be a problem for you if I sent money from time to time to help you pay your debt?" The son answered with great trust: "No, I wouldn't mind, Dad. I would never demand your help, but I do expect it because you're my dad and you love me." The father's heart was filled with joy. No presumption from the son; just simple faith that his father was behind him, loving him, helping in every and any way he could. God must take pleasure in our simple trust in Him; not presumptuously demanding of Him, but trustfully expecting, because we know He loves us. It is a trust that needs no demanding because we know His character, His trustworthy promises. Lord, teach us to trust You that way!

# June 7<sup>th</sup>
## Not Overpowered

"And the light shineth in darkness; and the darkness comprehended it not." John 1:5

In the midst of our despair, darkness, and desperation, the light shines, and the light shines in. Sometimes it is a crashing, blinding, thunderous flash of light that immediately releases us from our prison of blackness. Other times, it is just a candle flicker giving hope and guidance to lead us out. But above all, remember - the darkness will never overpower the light. Darkness creeps in, but it never completely dispels light - but light has the awesome ability to make its presence known even in the smallest quantity, while a little darkness cannot even gain attention in a light-filled room. No matter how dark your trial,

He is the light that can never go out.

# June 8<sup>th</sup>
# Quieting

"The Lord thy God in the midst of thee is mighty; he will save, he will rejoice over thee with joy; he will rest in his love, he will joy over thee with singing.." Zephaniah 3:17

In times of anxiousness, trouble or pain, we become desperate in our desire to have God speak to us. We flip from page to page in our Bible, looking for some special word. We pray fervently, hear nothing in return and say, "God, why won't you talk to me!"

Years ago, during a time of personal crisis with pressing decisions, a wise man of God spoke this precious word to me: "It's like a school science project where you add water to a jar or soil and then shake it. All you see a first is cloudy water. But just let it settle, then you will see layers form, and it will all be clear. You need to stop shaking the jar and let it settle before you can see God's will clearly."

When in difficult straits or painful circumstances, God's first priority is to quiet you in His love. Fear, panic, and anxiety may actually keep you from hearing His speaking. Only when you have stood still awaiting His salvation can He begin to settle things. Stop shaking the jar; patiently wait, resting in His love. He will make things clear in time.

# June 9<sup>th</sup>
## Help

"My voice shalt thou hear in the morning, O Lord; in the morning will I direct my prayer unto thee, and will look up." Psalm 5:3

Through the dark times, we know God is with us. But faith grows strongest in the dark, and God often withholds strong action on our behalf so we may glean those treasures from darkness. But, as one has said, God's hard word is not His last word - and upon seeing the first glimmer of dawn, you will experience the active blessing of God in great measure. That is the expectant hope that will see you through even the darkest hours.

# June 10<sup>th</sup>
## Good or Bad

"I could not go beyond the Word of the Lord, to do either good or bad of my own will." Numbers 24:13

This should always be the posture of the Lord's servant. Sometimes "good things" are not God's things - how many of us have taken upon ourselves a burden to help someone, only to have it end in spiritual calamity? Perhaps it was a good thing, but was it God's? To withhold evil when we really seek our own vengeance, or to refrain from even good when we know God's hand is not in it; this is the way of a true servant of a sovereign Lord.

# June 11<sup>th</sup>
## Power

"!And your eyes shall see, and ye shall say, The Lord will be magnified from the border of Israel." Malachi 1:5

We need a vision that extends beyond our borders. We are sheltered, warm and secure. Perhaps the reason many of us do not see great miracles is that we do not venture beyond the borders of our own securities. To us, a broken appliance is a trauma. Across the seas, a little girl is grateful to find a single herb to eat. In my travels to Europe, I forever had my limited vision shattered. In state churches baptism as an adult sometimes means expulsion, and there is no aliveness except in rare pockets here and there among the faithful. It extended my borders, and I took the world into my heart. We are a privileged people in material prospering, but a poor powerless people in our vision.

May God open our eyes to see the power of God beyond our borders. May we be bold to venture beyond our securities to see God's power among those who do not know yet of that great power and love.

# June 12<sup>th</sup>

"…they made me the keeper of the vineyards; but mine own vineyard have I not kept.." Song of Songs, 1:6b

Those of us who would serve others often neglect our own walk with God. We become consumed by the needs, burdens, and problems of others. Suddenly inflow of the Spirit decreases and our own outflow increases until we are dry, desolate and despondent. We have been so busy tending the vineyards of the needy that our own has become wasted. Jesus frequently retreated to fortify His communion with the Father. "Virtue has gone out of Me." Thus, it must be refilled. It is not selfish. It is needful. Otherwise, even our tending of others' vines will be in anger and frustration, bringing death rather than life. God desires each of us to come away into our own garden, and loving Him there, return with HIS strength!

# June 13th
## Honey

"He made him to draw honey from the rock."
Deuteronomy 32:13b

Hard circumstances are not meant to be only that. God has put within His people the power to take any circumstance and gain sweet treasure from it. If we become hardened and bitter because our circumstances are difficult, we will strike at that rock in anger like Moses, and rob ourselves of blessing from it.

There is honey in every rock-like circumstance in your life. By the power of the Holy Spirit, draw honey from that rock, strike it not in anger or frustration. Reflect on that rock, see it as God sees it; not an obstacle but a refiner; not a block, but a building stone; not a bitter stopping place but an opportunity to overcome. That which seems most hard, under His hand, can yield sweetness, growth, and life.

# June 14<sup>th</sup>
## Not God

"They have provoked Me to jealousy by what is not God." Deuteronomy 32:21a

We must dispense with the notion that God approves of everything bearing His Name. How easy it is to build, expand and move ahead, justifying it because of selfish ambitions. Many a lust and self-serving device have been passed under spiritual justification. Like Saul, we say, "I did it for God!" to avoid facing our own selfish motivations. God is jealous. Our priority must at all times be seeking His will, loving Him first.

Anything that robs us of intimacy and time with Him, any project that does not expressly promote the Gospel and God's glorification incites God's deep jealousy. Put all things under the naked light of Him with whom we have to do; determine not to move without the cloud by day or the fire by night.

# June 15<sup>th</sup>
## Spent Days

"So teach us to number our days, that we may apply our hearts unto wisdom." Psalm 90:12

Every new day before us is a potential. We can waste it on unimportant things. We can turn that into a habit, then a lifestyle. Or we can consciously commit the day to God upon waking: "Good morning, Father! What are YOU doing today - and can You use me?" For our earthly days are unexpectedly short. Some, by never recognizing that shortness, have frittered away an entire lifetime, ending up with hands full of chaff. Others, by inviting God to participate in each day's planning, have found their days filled with fruitful activity for Him. There are people needing love. There are hands needing strengthening. There are hearts needing mending. Take advantage of every moment for Him, knowing that life is always too short, and as one has wisely said, the only thing we take with us at death is what we have given away.

# June 16<sup>th</sup>
## Sovereignty

"Know ye that the Lord he is God: it is he that hath made us, and not we ourselves; we are his people, and the sheep of his pasture." Psalm 100:3

To the unknowing, the sovereignty of God is a fearful thing. The Lord is God" - in other words, "He can do anything - hurt me, neglect me, punish me." But to know Him as Father, "the Lord is God" are words of security and strength. I do not fear His sovereignty; in fact, it is my joyous hope in times of trouble! It means I am not alone or on my own. I am taken care of. I am His lamb, His responsibility. In His sovereignty lies my purest rest; for He who sees all would not let one hair of my head be banned. He loves me! Even when everything else seems out of control, I need not fear. I can sleep in sweet peace, knowing that He who rules the stars cares dearly for His little lamb, defenseless and trusting, safe in His gentle arms. Hallelujah!

# June 17<sup>th</sup>
## Home Front

"I will behave myself wisely in a perfect way. O when wilt thou come unto me? I will walk within my house with a perfect heart." Psalm 101:2

We are so brave and bold, so pure and noble to those who do not know us well! But the real cauldron, the supreme test of our walk with God is what comes out of us with those closest to our heart and home. It is a humiliation to the flesh to mightily proclaim God's Word to an outsider, then blow up in anger when our loved one irritates us. It is so easy to love those we do not live with! They ask little and often hold us in undue esteem. But I am convinced God has designed our home and loved ones as the iron to sharpen iron, the two-way mirror that shows us who we really are. As we learn to accept, face and overcome our home failures, we can then face those on the outside with greater confidence vulnerability and tangible humanity touched by the grace of God.

# June 18<sup>th</sup>
# Justifying

"But wisdom is justified by all her children." Luke 7:35

I prayed over this verse for many years without understanding. Life experience brought me a clear revelation. Jesus was dealing with a group of people who would not face the truth, and so could not face their own wicked hearts. They disliked John because he was too holy. They disliked Jesus because he ate with sinners. In other words, nothing could please them, because they cared not for the truth. They were so purposely blind, they did not even see their own contradictions. In other words, then, when a man runs from the truth, especially truth that pierces personally, he can then justify all his actions, thoughts and words as perfectly wise in his own eyes.

The Greek word for hypocrite is "play-actor." Like Saul of old, a classic play-actor, he could do what he pleased, blame who he would, never face himself, and yet felt perfectly justified in all he did. I have met such people, and I have been such a man. Unwilling to face the truth, life then becomes an endless series of blame-shifting, rationales, and justifications, one built to support the others. And after a while, one begins to believe one's own press releases, despite mounting contrary evidence! And all the while, it seems like "wisdom" to us! O God of all truth, help us to be honest people, David-like people, willing to face ourselves without justifying our every sinful action. Only then will the truth set us free.

# June 19th
# Honor

"Before honor is humility." Proverbs 15:33b

The scriptures tell us that he who desires leadership desires an honorable thing. But from desire to fulfillment lies a tested path many refuse to take. Joseph had a dream of leadership, but he was full of youthful pride and insecurity. It took many years of testing to prepare him for leadership. It was a time of great humility, and humiliation. But Joseph served where he was, as diligently in a dirty prison as- in the courts of Pharaoh. Humility before honor; purging before placement. On this path, God weeds out the human ambitions and the humanly ambitious.

Those desiring power without purging, authority before anointing and responsibility before release will either fall by the wayside, or take a place not given to them, thereby damaging many under them. It is better to accept God's way: humility before honor!

# June 20<sup>th</sup>
## Seekers

"This is the generation of them that seek Him..."
Psalms 24:6

We have entered history's most perilous time. It will no longer suffice to live a benign, inactive, comfortable Christian life. God is asking more. The forces of evil grow in strength. God is calling out with an increasingly urgent voice, "Seek Me while it is still day." He is seeking a generation, a handful, a remnant who have the courage to give up all the devices, manipulations and mechanics of modern day evangelistic thrust and admit that all our ways are powerless. It must be the divine anointing. He seeks those who will come stripped, broken and desperate, saying, "Lord, have mercy, we have failed. If you don't do the work, it will never get done!" It is that seeker God desires to pour His anointing onto. May God grant us the power to truly be that generation that seeks their Lord.

# June 21ˢᵗ
## Desolations

"Moreover I will take from them the voice of mirth, and the voice of gladness, the voice of the bridegroom, and the voice of the bride, the sound of the millstones, and the light of the candle." Jeremiah 25:10

When we turn from God to destructive or worldly influences, there's a progression of desolation that this verse reveals. First, we lose our joy and acceptance of God's life in us. Then, we stop hearing the voice of the Bridegroom: "Why can't I hear God anymore?" Next, we lose the voice of the bride - OUR voice, both of witness and prayer, as well as our ability to hear the Bride's voice, that of the counsel and care of other believers. Then all our "millstones" stand silent: we become nonproductive, fruitless. Finally, the light of truth and direction are snuffed out, leaving us in darkness and despair. If you've come to this place, the way back is clearly marked. Start up this ladder a step at a time. Restore the candle first: "Thy Word is a lamp unto my feet and light unto my path." (Ps. 119) Let His Word heal and strengthen you. Then "do the first works." (Rev.1) Get the millstone going again. Make the Word, prayer and fellowship a priority. Soon the millstones of faith will begin to turn again. Then let the Bride be heard - the counsel of loved believers and your own voice, your pleadings for restoration be heard before God's throne once more. Next, listen; you have begun building again, and you will once more hear the Bridegroom's voice saying, "This is the Way, walk ye in it." The crown and seal of every completed work of God will strengthen you in your every step. "Remember from whence you are fallen." The way home must always begin by retracing our steps.

# 22<sup>nd</sup>
# Hidden Path

"Thy way is in the sea, and thy path in the great waters, and thy footsteps are not known." Psalm 77:19

Are you facing an impossible situation? God knows. He loves impossible situations, for He is the God of all possibilities. Do you see no way out? There is a door! You may not see it. It is likely a door you could not have seen, and would never have imagined. Our God is the God of Joseph, who took him from prison to Pharaoh's court through a dream of Pharaoh's, and through a man who remembered there was a dream interpreter in prison named Joseph. Our God is the God of Moses, who placed him before the impossible door of the Red Sea and then opened a door right through it! God often waits until we cannot open any more doors ourselves until there is no visible path, only faith. Then you will be surprised by joy as He makes a way where no way is! Trust Him! He sees that which no human eye can see. His light will show you the way out of the impossible.

# June 23rd
## Listening and Conquering

"Oh that my people had hearkened unto me, and Israel had walked in my ways! I should soon have subdued their enemies, and turned my hand against their adversaries." Psalm 81:13-14

Listening and following are the keys to freedom. Listening to God's Word, listening to the loving counsel of friends and elders, listening to the still small voice of the Holy Spirit. Have you taken time to listen to Him, or are you merely running from your struggles, hoping they will somehow go away? Or are you running to books, tapes or worldly advice for help? God's Word and voice are personal but are only heard by those who TAKE TIME to hear Him. Then when you hear you must FOLLOW. God's Word is one big action word: Follow Me. Preach My Word. Give to the poor.

Care for the widows and orphans. Crucify the flesh. To hear is important, but it is useless unless you follow what you have heard!

To hear and follow opens the prison door to let you go free.

# June 24<sup>th</sup>
## The Danger of Complaining

"And they tempted God in their heart by asking meat for their lust.." Psalm 78:18

There is nothing more deadly spiritually than an ungrateful heart, lusting for more than God has given. God has given us all we need in His Word, His Family, and His Presence. When His Word begins to bore you, when fellowship irritates you and His presence escapes you, then you are in a place of great danger, for then the tempter comes and says, "Aren't you tired of the struggle? The world has so much to offer you!" Suddenly your eyes see things you lust to have, and lusts you have buried are suddenly unearthed, come back from the edge of this dangerous cliff. Come to your senses! Satan had an open door to your heart because of your own ungrateful heart. Thank God for all you have, all He has given and continues to give you. He will not deprive you of one good thing if you develop a thankful heart.

A thankful heart moves God's heart to give. An ungrateful heart stings His great Heart and forces Him to let you pursue your own evil desires.

# June 25th
## Possessions

"Honor the Lord with your possessions." Proverbs 3:9a

I believe this not only speaks of giving God what we have but making sure everything we have honors Him. It is good to take inventory of the things we own. Do we keep books or magazines that are questionable? Do we watch certain T.V. shows for purely sensual reasons? I have met Christians who would never be caught in gross sin, yet have zodiac signs, Buddhas, good luck charms or even a "kitchen witch," without thought to its danger. We are known by our possessions as well as our professions. We should not hesitate to discard anything not honorable to God.

# June 26<sup>th</sup>
## Still In My Heart

"And the children of Benjamin did not drive out the Jebusites that inhabited Jerusalem, but the Jebusites dwelt with the children of Jerusalem to this day." Judges 1:21

There are sins so obvious that we must battle them and win or we will die; fornication, drunkenness, hate, and bitterness. They are obvious to everyone and unmistakably destructive.

But some sins are "small" enough and "innocent" enough and sneaky enough to just hide in a dark closet of our heart unnoticed by others and ignored by ourselves. Sins like pride, gossip, cowardice, laziness, cheating and such, will remain firmly planted in us if we allow it. Because they are not as obvious as the "big" sins, it becomes too easy to put off dealing with them, brushing off the stinging of our conscience that says we MUST deal with them. Because we do not drive them out (which means a no-kidding, violent assault) they continue to dwell in us, and while we may not want to believe they are having major consequences on us, nonetheless they are creating confusion, spiritual failure and robbing you of present usefulness and future joys.

Have the guts to face the truth. Pray, "Lord, leave no enemy in me not fought and not exposed. Destroy them all." You will first be shocked to realize the "little" sins were big destroyers after all, and then, you will experience incredible growth and power after they have been uprooted.

# June 27th
## Turned Backs

"...and behold, at the door of the temple of the Lord, between the porch and the altar, were...men, with their backs turned toward the temple of the Lord..." Ezekiel 8:16

Jeremiah, the great heartbroken Prophet, wept between the porch and the altar, praying to God for His people. This is our call. This is the mark of a true Shepherd of God. But what do we find now? God's priests, God's "prophets," turning their backs on the temple of prayer and losing their power and compassion. Before good works, before ministry, before anything else, you must learn communion and intercession with God. To lose that is to lose the power to do all else.

What has caused you to turn your back on the temple? Busyness? Worries? A non-stop counseling schedule? Let it all go - no, make it fall back in line and give way to the one priority you must maintain to be God's effective servant, the place of His Presence. Make it first in your day. All else will be well.

# June 28<sup>th</sup>
## Study

"The heart of the righteous studies how to answer."
Proverbs 15:28

Those of us who desire to help the hurting, correct the contentious and teach the troubled must not be so anxious to help that we hastily give answers. There is a fit word for every person and problem. It may not be the same answer for all. The wise counselor first listens, then waits, studying the matter in his spirit. He consults the Holy Spirit, asking for His perfect counsel. Only at the last does he speak. Only the foolish come prepared with standard answers and pet verses. You may thus damage when you meant to deliver, hurt when you meant to heal.

Remember that HE is the wonderful counselor; you are but a mouthpiece for Him. Wait for His Word; study to answer, then speak in His confident anointing.

# June 29<sup>th</sup>
## Beyond Salvation

"Therefore, behold, the days shall come, saith the Lord, that they shall no more say, 'The Lord lives, which brought up the children of Israel out of the land of Egypt," but, "The Lord lives, which brought up and which led the seed of the house of Israel out of the North country, and from all the countries where I had driven them; and they shall dwell in their own land. '" Jeremiah 23:8

This passage is rich with the ways of God with His children. First, it speaks hope to those who, having been saved, think that is all there is: God saves me, now I must struggle and fend for myself. No! God doesn't just "bring us up out of our past" but also *leads us on!* The God who delivered Israel out of Egypt with a mighty hand also gave them many miracles and a pillar of smoke and fire to lead them through the wilderness.

Second, God's intent is not to stop at our "bringing out" but also "bringing to." We are going somewhere! Before Christ, we were slaves, owned, property of evil. Much of God's work in us now is to "drive out the enemy" within us, so we can "dwell in our own land" — a life free from outside forces, inside torment and alien possession — free to serve Him fully in possession of our lives under His loving Rule.

# June 30th
# Expression

In the beginning was the Word, and the Word was with God, and the Word was God. " John 1:1

Creation...communication...communion — these things are in our Father's heart. He desires to express Himself still to His people whom He made to be like Him. He is a creator, and He put a creative desire in His children. Revelation says for His pleasure things were and *are* created. He is still creating and desires to create in and through *us*. Like an artist. His creation tells us much about who He is. He is a lover of beauty, and of the majestic. He expresses who He is in all His creation.

*Communication...* Just as we crave to communicate who we are to others, so does our Father. Every page of Holy Writ pleads, "Let Me tell you who I am!" He has expressed Himself, by the communication of His Word, and desires for us to know Him there daily.

*Communion...* More is said in the silent embrace of two lovers than in a volume of words. It is communion that needs no words. It is one that expresses and fulfills one's deepest longings. In all our prayers, let us be mindful to commune with our eternal Lover in the silence of love. It is perhaps in this silence of Holy Communion that He expresses Himself the deepest, that we know Him the best and receive from Him the fullest.

# July 1st
## Sorrow

"They reward me evil for good, to the sorrow of my soul." Psalm 35:12

I believe one of the greatest tests of Christian character comes in the agony of rejected kindness, of bitter rejection of good done. And it is often much easier to release those who have rejected our kindnesses, if they are unbelievers or distant acquaintances. The real test comes, as it did for David, when a "familiar friend," one we have loved and nurtured, lifts up their heel against us. It hurts! And we must make a choice concerning that hurt. Unconditional love is the highest goal, but when our soul, our emotions, our affections have been mortally wounded, it is then we discover how little we know of Christ-like love and forgiveness. We can easily release an unbeliever who rejects us because they were not close enough to wound us. But those we trusted and invested in — when they turn from, or on us, it is an impossible task in our flesh to forgive and release. Unconditional love then must be a work of grace in such a case. In our own flesh, we would defend ourselves, lash out, build walls, tell others of injustices. But we can choose - and indeed there is but one choice to make if we would be like Him - to let God show us how to love and forgive without expecting a return. In a great wounding, that work of grace not only releases the one who wounded; it keeps us open, saying, "I choose to love you, and if necessary, will let you wound me again." A person who dares make that vulnerable choice will experience grace beyond any human ability to love - and to forgive.

# July 2nd
# Upward

"The way of life winds upward for the wise, that he may turn away from hell below." Proverbs 15:24

Saint of God, you often wonder if all of life is an uphill climb. It is! Our walk with Him is a journey to the Heights. Those who never have an upward turn spend their spiritual lives enmeshed in the things of this world, the cares of this life, and attractions of the flesh. We are by nature a people who prefer the lowlands, the plains of plenty and the comfort of ease. Not so for the child of God; in each of us, there is a yearning, a restlessness for more. The bold will beseech God for the journey, no longer content with the "safe places." The journey upward means thinner air, but stronger lungs; discipline of heart, but clarity of vision. The higher the climb, the more we will of necessity discard, one by one, the encumbrances of this world, the weights of sin from the world below. And along the way, there are pools of refreshment, scenes of majesty and unknown provisions the Valley People never know of. And once resolved to the climb, may we give it our all until the summit, and may our final words be, "O let me climb when I lay down!" (Vaughan, 1622-1695)

Through the battle...
Through defeat...
Moving yet, and never stopping.
Pioneers! O! Pioneers!
- Whitman

# July 3<sup>rd</sup>
## Commitment

"If I perish, I perish." (Esther 4:15b)

There is a depth of commitment that comes to every believer who is determined to follow on. It comes when all that is past is ashes, and all that is to come is uncertain, and all that is now is shaky. God brings you to new decisions to go on, new revelation of the Cost of Following. You know that to go back would be betrayal, yet what is ahead? What promise is there that you will not fail, that blessing, not death, await you? God gives you none of that; only this: "I will never leave you nor forsake you." So we surrender. "If I perish, I perish." Suddenly, the prospect of life is no longer meaningful if we can't move forward, upward. "Whatever, God. I'd rather die than not know Your Presence." And His Presence is always in our next step - not with those who sit complacently, never risking the Journey.

# July 4<sup>th</sup>
## Fear Of Suffering

"Now you too have been of no help; you see something dreadful and are afraid." (Job 6:21)

In Job's sufferings, his friends came with tears and compassion, but the horror of his loss frightened them. That's when they began to talk, to come up with explanations for his pain. Their words were of no help because they came from fear. The pain that comes upon the innocent reflects like a mirror back to us, and we think, "If they weren't spared, what about me?" That fear - of being vulnerable to tragedy no matter how rightly we live - causes us to find reasons (surely there must be reasons!) why this person has been afflicted (and so, why we won't be.) Sin in their life. Lack of faith!

Only the brave will face the mirror of another's' pain and reach beyond it, knowing the rain does fall on the just and the unjust, knowing what they need most is not our fearful explanations but our silent love, our walking beside.

# July 5<sup>th</sup>
## Keeping Track

"Surely then You will count my steps but not keep track of my sin." (Job 14:16)

What is God most interested in? It is in our fearful, human nature to assume God is writing down every failure, every sin, and it's all written in permanent ink! But His real interest is in our <u>steps</u>, not our <u>sins</u>. That's what He watches most lovingly; for He knows our steps toward Him can break the power of every sin. He deals with sin only because it cripples our <u>steps</u>. Like a proud parent whose child has learned to walk, they don't write down, "My child fell five times today; at five o'clock, seven o'clock," and so on. But they will write and remember and tell anyone who is near, "My child walked today!" So it is with our steps. So it will be all our days. Such a loving memory God has; to remember our growth and forget our failures.

# July 6<sup>th</sup>
## Heartache

"Yet if I speak, my pain is not relieved; if I refrain, it does not go away." (Job 16:6)

Have you ever walked through this kind of heartache? It is so deep, so profound that nothing can touch it, nothing helps. I have often felt such pain. Keeping silent only makes the pain louder, sharper and inescapable; yet talking about it only makes you aware of how real it is, how big and how unmovable. To be alone is hell, to be with a friend is worse. There is no escape, even in the night!

If God ever lets you walk through this kind of pain, know that only two things are sure: He knows and feels your heartache; and He has allowed it because He knows the outcome is worth the suffering; you will come out the other side purer, more gentle and compassionate, surer of His good love and more secure than ever before. It is the way of God with His chosen beloved children.

# July 7<sup>th</sup>
# Change

" For I am now ready to be offered, and the time of my departure is at hand." 2 Timothy 4:6

Paul, nearly at the end of his human life, speaks of the change from his earthly body to eternal life. He was ready. The "finishing touch" was almost complete.

Like a fine sculpture, God takes the raw clay of our life when we are redeemed, then begins molding us, shaping us, breaking, reshaping. Often we do not see what He's making as we "spin on the potter's wheel." No matter; He is skilled. He knows the finished product. He sees it before it is begun, and we are beautiful to Him even in our most unredeemed state, for He knows what we will become.

May God give you the grace to endure the molding, through the polishing stage of your life, the Finishing Touch of His Hand as He adds His final colors, shape, and glory. May you see, even now, a glimpse of the Glory to be and what you will become under His Hand.

# July 8<sup>th</sup>
## Strength

"Save me, O God, by Thy Name, and judge me by Thy strength." (Psalm 54:1)

Aren't you glad God judges us by His strength? When a child learning to walk falls, a loving parent doesn't get angry because he doesn't walk like an adult. He's still a child. The parent judges the child's progress according to the parent's standing, knowing a child only walks by patient effort, sometimes failing, but always, always the parent encourages, picks up, gives another chance. That is our Father's heart too. Don't fear; He knows our frame and remembers we are but dust. He only asks that we stand after falling and continue to follow His steps.

# July 9th
## Light of the World

"As long as I am in the world, I am the Light of the world." (John 9:5)

Jesus is no longer bodily in this world. While He was, "the people in darkness saw a great light." When He left, He gave *us* that Light. It is the Presence of Himself in us by the Holy Spirit. Now we are the light of the world. What an awesome trust, and such an incredible responsibility! Think of it: everywhere we go, Light goes. You can try to hide it, ignore it, cover it with a barrel; still, if we do, people somehow know. Even a hidden light makes people turn their head and wonder who we are, because the Light of Jesus in us, even hidden, is weighty and intense and cannot really be concealed. Better by far to LET IT SHINE. It's not about words. It's about us being light-transformed people whose mere presence brings healing and power.

I long for the day that we are once more so free and transparent that people say, "You're different. Why?" Do you remember?

# July 10<sup>th</sup>
## Adversities

"Thou has known my soul in adversities." (Psalm 31:7a)

They say you only really know a person's true heart in difficulties and pressures. Then, what is in the heart will surface. An example of this is when patients undergo surgery. Doctors and Nurses tell me that when the patient comes out of surgery and the anesthetic begins to wear off, families are often shocked to find their loved one cursing, angry, rude and abusive. Then, some come out smiling, grateful, at peace, speaking words of love to their loved ones. The pain and the anesthetic have discovered and brought out what was in their heart of hearts.

In the heat of trials and sorrows, Jesus "knows" our souls; He brings out that hidden heart. There is no hiding. He sees us. We will, too. God isn't interested in your religious acts and surface show; He wants to know the real heart of you and love you as you are, and adversity cuts to the center so He may know us unhindered by pretense. Thank Him for it! He comes to our hidden soul, and finds us, and lets us know He is Lord of all He finds in that place, good or bad.

# July 11<sup>th</sup>
## God's Classroom

"What man is he that feareth the Lord? Him shall He teach in the way that He shall choose." (Psalm 26:12)

In helping others, you must be very careful to let the Holy Spirit be the Teacher. We are all in different stages of spiritual growth, and the Holy Spirit uniquely tailors His classroom for each soul according to their history, gifts, sensitivities, vulnerabilities, and willingness. You will be tempted to say, "Well, God must do it <u>this</u> way, like He did with me," or "You cannot do it this way, because I did not." The Holy Spirit is a jealous Teacher, and I recommend you be His teacher's assistant and leave the methods and timing to Him. He will teach them in the way HE shall choose.

# July 12<sup>th</sup>
# Serving

" After that he poureth water into a bason, and began to wash the disciples' feet." John 13:5a

"Do you understand what I have done to you?" (John 13:12b)

There may be a treasure of reasons and lessons we've yet to discover in Jesus' example of foot washing. One that is rarely understood is this: It's so unlike the world! The world grasps for power, for wealth, for position. It is selfish, self-serving and uses others merely as a stepping-stone to a greater place of self-importance. Jesus says you say you are Mine; then serve and wash each other's' feet with disregard, even dislike for personal reward or position. Like a blinding flash of lightning, such acts of serving will expose the completely selfish hearts of the world and be better proof that we are not of the world than a thousand eloquent sermons. Our servanthood will shock and wound the world which has grown to expect religious folks to be just as selfish - if not more - than them. It will be a powerful proof that He lives in us in power.

# July 13<sup>th</sup>
## Messengers

" Verily, verily, I say unto you, He that receiveth whomsoever I send receiveth me..." John 13:20a

I wonder how often we fail to hear His Voice because we reject His messenger. Remember that Israel cried for Messiah to come then killed Him because He did not come in King's clothes. We will hear people of importance, influence, and power, of wealth and social equality or superiority. But what if God sent a child, or a street beggar, or even a sinner? Impossible? Yet God spoke both through a prophet's donkey and High Priest Caiaphas, the first a laughable mouthpiece and the second a Christ-killer. WHO God speaks through is His business; ours is to be humble enough and close enough to His Heart that we are willing and able to hear Him regardless of who He sends. To refuse to do so because of the messengers' appearance or age or social condition is to risk rejecting Jesus Himself.

# July 14th
## Go-Betweens

" Now there was leaning on Jesus' bosom one of his disciples, whom Jesus loved. Simon Peter therefore beckoned to him, that he should ask who it should be of whom he spake. John 13:24

Peter asked John to be a go-between for him with Jesus. At the time, Peter was concerned with correctness, power, religious things. John just loved Jesus. That is why John was the closest to Jesus because he just loved Him, which is what Jesus wanted from all of them. I think Peter, too, could have leaned on Jesus' breast, but his preoccupation with outward things prevented such intimate longing for a place near the Master's Heart.

And so, like many of us, he was left with asking those who were close to Jesus what His thoughts were. We want our pastor, priest, or counselor to talk to Jesus for us. "Pray for me." You do not realize; you may go to Him just as John! It's important to ask for prayer, but you must also know that you need no go-between. Jesus longs to share His thoughts and His heart with you. But you must let go of your dependency and desire for a go-between and enter in yourself, knowing that you, too are "the disciple that Jesus loved," if you would only love Him back.

# July 15<sup>th</sup>
## Peace

" Saying, If thou hadst known, even thou, at least in this thy day, the things which belong unto thy peace! but now they are hid from thine eyes." Luke 19:42

We think of peace as the absence of trouble, strife, war. We think of it as the condition in which life is one big rosebush, with no thorns. We want it to be a meadow with all flowers and no rocks.

But for the believer, what are the "conditions of peace"? When we are saved, God first strips us of the illusion that peace is external at all. Instead of an end to war, we are put in a battle. Instead of everything going our way, life becomes a minefield of obstacles.

The conditions for peace - for us - are internal. "Not as the world gives, I give you peace," He says. So the world's peace is the absence of war and strife. His peace is the ability to be calm and at rest even in the midst of the severest battles we will ever face. It is not the absence of war. It is knowing the victory of our Captain. It is not the ease of circumstances. It is not to be moved by even the harshest of circumstances. It is far better to be a tempered steel vessel that can go into the hottest fires than the fragile vase which can hold flowers but cannot withstand one crack.

# July 16<sup>th</sup>
## Ultimate Security

"The Lord is the portion of mine inheritance and of my cup; thou maintainest my lot." (Psalm 16:5)

No matter what my "lot" - no matter how I strive for earthly security, financial freedom and prosperity, emotional support - God alone maintains my life. God deliver me from striving for those things at all. Let me know that He alone is my indestructible portion. Only He remains. Banks will fail, fortunes will come and go, friends will change and sometimes drift away - but God has given me a lifetime of spiritual resources, built a fence around it and said, "This is My own. I will not allow it to be taken from Me." It is the ultimate security. He will not leave me a desolate lot; He will not leave me an orphan; He will come to me. I cannot lose Him - the real inheritance, the only one worth anything at all. Let it all be taken, all the riches and relationships - I have Him still, and He is all I want or need.

# July 17th
## Joy

"In Thy Presence is fullness of joy." (Psalm 16:11)

What really brings joy? I've prospered, I've been poor. I've been homeless and lived in great comfort. I've been honored, humiliated, beloved and friendless, fulfilled and empty. Emotions change; people change, circumstances change. In it all, I know only one thing matters: His Presence. It is the only Place where I can rise above my pain or heartache, any betrayal or loss, and come out with joy - not an emotional high, but true contentment, a settling, a knowing that all is well. God, ever give me Your Presence. Without it, I am just a little boat on a troubled and dangerous sea. With it, I am an unsinkable buoy, with the unmovable anchor of Your Heart.

# July 18th
# A Small Shield

"He is a buckler to those who trust in Him." (Psalm 18:30)

Buckler here means "small shield". It is greatly comforting to know God has provided not just a great protection against great attacks, but also a "small shield" for the more numerous - and more tiring and draining - small attacks from Satan. For ultimately, soldiers in this battle are not often laid low by the big attacks, but by the constant little ones, draining our strength and taking our attention from Him. Thank God, today I can raise that small shield too and be safe from them all.

# July 19<sup>th</sup>
## Striving

"Thou hast delivered me from the strivings of the people." (Psalm 18:43)

One of the greatest gifts God can give those who love Him, especially those called to serve, is to be freed from trying to be someone else. To be free from jealousy, envy, feeling "less than", to be liberated from fighting for position, prestige, recognition - what a peace! "Just content to be a son." The striving to "be somebody", to gain the acclaim and praise of others, is an empty and unfulfilling quest. How much power is enough? How much recognition satisfies? To be satisfied just that He knows and loves us, and has given us a place HE has chosen (no matter how small it may seem to us), that is freedom. That is fulfillment at its highest.

# July 20<sup>th</sup>
# Darkness

"He made darkness His secret place." (Psalm 18:11a)

In each of us there are things we hide in darkness, things that shame us, frighten us...things we cannot tell another for fear of rejection...things so wrong, so ugly that we prefer to keep them locked away and only see them when they threaten to overcome us and ruin our lives. Past sins...unexpected impulses...secret desires we yield to when no one sees...how frightening, how crippling they are!

But Jesus is already there! When we get honest enough to open the door on that dark room and say, "Lord, I can't take this! Search it out! Destroy this thing that hides so well!", He is already there, for in that very darkness, He has made His secret place, a place He already knew of because He waits there with Light, waiting to expose it and free us from it grip! He is not ashamed of us there; His love is greater than this dark enemy. Like a skilled surgeon, He awaits our permission to cut out the cancerous sin, but first He awaits our acknowledgment of its presence and our powerlessness over it. Don't run from the dark sins hiding. He is there. He will set you free!

# July 21st
## Light

"For You will light my candle; the Lord my God will enlighten my darkness." (Psalm 18:28)

Are you struggling with things you don't understand? Is there an internal fight with feelings, reactions, and sins that seem to compel you and you don't know why? Does confusion of thought, emotional trouble, and spiritual battle make you want to give up? "I don't understand God. I don't understand myself or others. What's wrong with me?"

Even though our salvation is immediate and sure when we invite Jesus into our hearts, He's got a lot of junk to clean out. There are a lot of dark places and things Past hiding there; hidden wounds, silent injuries that hang on like death and push us into more hurt.

Over the years, this prayer has been an open door into my heart: "God, bring to light whatever is in darkness in me." David said, "Search me, O God." (Psalm 139) God knows what we cannot see, and when we ask, He does shed His searchlight on the dark places of our hearts. He does it not to hurt, but heal. If we do not see, we cannot be free. Once we see the hidden sin or hurt that is buried for what it is, we can yield it and ask Him to crucify it and replace it with light and new life. He will enlighten our darkness.

# July 22nd
## Above

"Lift up your head, o ye gates, and be lift up, ye everlasting doors; and the King of Glory shall come in." (Psalm 24:7)

How many times, when we're struggling, will someone dismiss our trouble with a quick, "Just look to Jesus!" or, "Just keep your eyes on God!" It neither helps nor comes with understanding from the one who tells us. But the truth of it is profound: When troubles surround us, there is no help in the sea of trouble! There are no solutions to be found by looking for one among the attacking troubles. We MUST raise our eyes ABOVE our circumstances and pain which are drowning and confusing us, to Jesus who is high and lifted up above them all. But this is not just some stoic act of keeping a "stiff upper lip." Something happens when we raise our eyes: In lifting our head and our heart to Him in a moment of anguish and desperation, suddenly the GATES of our heart, mind, and spirit are open, and He comes in, in His Power and Presence! The lifted gaze of our whole heart is an invitation the Master responds to, and He comes into our troubles to show us what to do, give us courage and fill us with His peaceful love.

# July 23rd
## Pleasure

"Thou shalt make them drink of the rivers of Thy pleasures." (Psalm 36:8a)

One of Satan's greatest deceptions is convincing people that following Jesus means giving up pleasure. What a lie! Yes, Satan is a great imitator, but if the counterfeit "pleasure" is so "pleasing" then the true is so much more so! The difference is, Satan's pleasures have a deadly price. The hangover follows the drunken night and the habit becomes an addiction. The sexual encounter is followed by guilt, broken relationships, and sometimes disease and death. Being your own pleasure-seeking god turns you into a miserable, lonely little fraud, friendless and unsatisfied. We sin because "there is pleasure in sin for a season." (Proverbs) We wouldn't do it if it didn't feel good or wasn't pleasurable. We choose to ignore the deadly hook in the bait.

But there is true pleasure in the Father's Gift Room, one that has no price tag nor penalty. Sex as God made it, in marriage, is pleasure-filled, intimate and cements a life of belonging, children, and peace. The Presence of God's Spirit brings a "drunkenness" of pure joy and freedom no drug or alcohol can compare with. True praise and worship are a party beyond description.

Pleasure? You can keep the world's version if you want. Having known the real thing, I'd never settle for the world's version. They have no idea what they're missing!

# July 24<sup>th</sup>
# Flourishing

"Those that be planted in the house of the Lord shall flourish in the courts of our God." (Psalm 92:13)

How do you make your daily life count? How do you stay strong, keep perspective and make a difference in the everyday circumstances of your life, the "unspiritual" (is anything really not touched by the spiritual?) things? This verse helps. Be planted and begin to root with those God gave you to pray with, worship with, grow with. The "house of the Lord" - that unique place of fellowship (flawed though it may be) is His shelter in this evil storm - drink of it! Use it! Absorb every tender touch and loving moment with others. Let your roots take every bit of strength from Jesus in those around you, from what you receive, what you give, what you learn. Soon those roots will spread, and your branches will flourish - and every "outside" thing and place, yes, every place, will become the "courts of our God," and you shall no longer see a separation but only a continuation of His grace to be a healing tree everywhere you go.

# July 25<sup>th</sup>
## Numbering

"So teach us to number our days, that we may apply our hearts unto wisdom." (Psalm 90:12)

Lately, I've been thinking about the shortness of this life. Leonard Ravenhill talks about us being a heartbeat away from a fixed, eternal state of reward. That makes me tremble, not because I long for a reward, nor fear hell, but simply because for Christians, for me, this life is a once in eternity opportunity. If I fear death, it is not out of insecurity about my salvation, but the thought of a lost chance to be all I can in this life. How can I explain it? The Great Olympic Games of Heaven, a chance to run, to obtain, to win the crown. I'm moved to the fight because the obstacles of sin and weakness are against me; people fail around me; yet He gave His Spirit and said, "You CAN fight a good fight; you CAN keep the faith!"

O Lord, help me to number my days, to realize this opportunity to be a Giant in the Lord will not come again. Let me realize how short life is so I can apply my heart to wisdom; in other words, to know what to cling to and what to discard, how to best spend my time, my energies, my strength, knowing that all things pass, all things burn away except what is built on eternal things!

# July 26<sup>th</sup>
## Fresh Oil

"I shall be anointed with fresh oil." (Psalm 92:10b)

I don't want to see the glorious works of my past; I want to see the new thing He will do. Every time (usually from spiritual laziness) I resort to old ways of doing things or talking to people, it fails. He that is Yesterday, Today and Forever longs to do a new thing in me, through me. Lord, I'm hungry for Today's Bread, not yesterday's. I long for fresh oil, fresh anointing! Let today be the beginning of that new thing; help me to let go of what could have been or what was, and hold out childlike hands with an excited heart that says, "God can do anything today! And He can do it through me!"

# July 27th
## Floods

"The floods have lifted up, O Lord, the floods have lifted up their voice..." (Psalm 93:3a)

"The Lord on high is mightier than the noise of many waters." (Psalm 93:4a)

I have a picture in my mind. It is of a mighty waterfall. To be near it is to be deafened by its roar. To be under it is to be overwhelmed with noise and violence so that nothing else is known. But on the other side, if you dive down and under it, is a grotto, a cave of shelter, where the roaring nearly ceases and it is almost calm.

The floods of strife and confusion, the noise of doubts and fears can come close to overwhelming us, so that nothing else is seen or heard, and one fears for their very spiritual life. But there is a place beyond the noise, a sheltering Grotto where all is at rest. It is His Presence. You hear His Voice! Turn, then, dive deeply into His Word and His Love; come apart from the human chatter and the strife of tongues, lay in His Presence and KNOW the Peace of God. You will hear His Voice there and know His comfort. He is mightier than the noisy waters just beyond. Dwell in that Hiding Place, and all will be well, every day, whatever floods may come.

# July 28<sup>th</sup>
## Not Taken Away

"I said, O my God, take me not away in the midst of my days." (Psalm 102:24)

A powerful fear grips a Christian when God gives a full glimpse of the shortness of life. If your heart is really set on eternity, there is no crying for the end of it all, no pitiful longing for heaven as an escape from earth - there is rather a shock, a realization that at best, there are not enough earthly days here to serve, to love, to see God manifested in a way that is unique in all eternity! This will not come again! Only once in eternity are we given to fight this battle, face down sin and rescue the lost, only once in eternity are we given the chance to obtain a crown, to oppose the devil and contest him for the lives of the prisoners and brokenhearted. Can't you see? IT WILL NOT COME AGAIN! Our hours of self-pity, looking for an easy out are wasting precious eternal moments of opportunity! So while I long at times to be Home with Him, I know NOW I am home IN Him, and I cry for length of days, for more precious time to be all He planned, do all He says and fight the battle of a Warrior who knows for this battle he was born!

# July 29th
# Writing

"This shall be written for the generation to come."
(Psalm 102: 18a)

All of us are "writing" something with our lives. Our life is a spiritual story. At the end, what will it say? What will the title of the book be? "He lived for himself alone." "She was a prisoner of her past." "They loved the world more than Jesus." "He ran from God's call." What will it be? Oh Father, let none of these be written! Let it be rather, "He finished the course." "She gave her heart to all who were hurting." "They cared for the orphan and the lonely."

God has given you the blank pages, the writing instruments and the time. He has provided all you need to write a glorious book of your life you can pass on to the next generation. But what is written is up to you alone. You can write a thin, selfish little volume filled with emptiness and shallow thoughts, or a full and rich living chronicle of Jesus Christ alive in you.

The next generation of readers awaits your decision!

# July 30<sup>th</sup>
## Eyes

"I will set no wicked thing before my eyes." (Psalm 101:3)

Before a sin grabs your heart, it usually passes our eyes, doesn't it? John speaks of "the lust of the eyes." In our media-obsessed day, we are daily barraged with sights and sounds of ungodly temptations, from barely clothed bodies to the car you'd do anything to own.

The more television and movies you watch, the more tormented your soul may be, because you are setting before your carnal heart a thousand evil images that say, "See, you could have this if only you weren't a Christian." Pornography, violent movies, etc. are all cheap ways to bypass God and get what we lust for without actually acting out the sin and lust on another person. But we suffer spirit and mind because we're cutting off grace to fulfill us with good things, and we eventually resent God for what we don't or can't have. Lust leads to lust. Are your eyes the gateway to evil lusts? Is it worth the torment and frustration? Turn away from those images. Set nothing wicked before you, and you will be free.

# July 31<sup>st</sup>
# Glory

"When the Lord shall build up Zion, He shall appear in His glory." (Psalm 102:16)

There are times when we are dry, lonely and wrecked. All the excitement and miracles of our early days with Jesus seem to be gone. We are left faced with ourselves - A full glimpse of sins' ravages in our heart and our own weaknesses, and we wonder if He will ever come to us again like before.

Take courage - He hasn't left you! It's necessary. You can't live on the outer abiding of the Holy Spirit's glory, like in the Old Testament, where He came, set on a man, did marvelous things, then left. Jesus wants more. He wants His glory and power to be a daily, steady, stable Presence in your life. But it comes now from the inside out. And first, He must begin to "rebuild Zion" - build you inside, renovate you, make full room for Jesus to be at home in your heart, with no locked doors. THEN He shall appear in His glory, and the Power and Grace of Jesus in you will pour FROM you as naturally as water down a waterfall. Let Him build you!

# August 1st
# Depths

"So He led them through the depths, as through the wilderness." (Psalm 106:96)

We are a nation of shallow Christians and soft faith. Most would be perfectly content to "side-slide" into heaven without being bothered or rocked. Not so the Way of God's Warriors. For those who dare to want His All for their lives, He leads them through the Depths. And it is as through a wilderness. Depth of power and strength, understanding and love do not come from the selfish places of ease and good feelings, but when we abandon easy choices and ask for His Ways. The Wilderness comes, where His face is obscured, and our faith is established, and in dry and difficult deserts we feel the reality of His Hand. From dryness comes depth, for under each wilderness, the Stream of Living Waters flows. In each dry test and difficult desert, He will bring forth a spiritual depth in you the Shallow Dwellers will never know, depths that bring abundance of unshakable love, abiding peace and unmovable joy.

It is worth it all!

# August 2nd
## Seeing the Good

"...that I may see the good of Thy Chosen." (Psalm 106:5a)

Some of Satan's most destructive acts come through gossip, slander and vicious division among Christians. But the heart of the servant says, "Show me the good."

God allows us to see the faults and sins in others for one reason alone: that we might pray for their deliverance. If it goes beyond that to become food for gossip, we have made it an evil thing.

If that is all we saw, we could be easily disheartened. "Lord, Christians are so messed up! All I see are the sins and wounds!" But look deeper; ask to "see the good of His Chosen." To see with Jesus' eyes another struggling servant means you see through the dirt and ugly things to the heart of hearts where Jesus Himself dwells, and you understand the precious nature of that soul, the goodness and unique specialness of the one He redeemed. When you see, not as much what they are in present struggles and sins, but what they will become through His love (aided by your unjudgmental prayers) they you fight for them - not against them - you begin to bear their burdens, you begin to cry out to God for them until Christ be fully formed in them.

# August 3rd
# Rocks

"He opened the rock, and the waters gushed out."
(Psalm 105: 41)

What is the hardest circumstance in your life right now? God's promise remains true; out of the rock shall come life to your spirit. God does not change rocks into pillows. He never softens the reality or substance of that rock of hardship. Rather, He promises if you face and strike that circumstance with the rod of faith in His goodness, if you confidently expect good to come from the center of it, life-giving refreshment of His Spirit will gush forth. I don't pray for the removal of rocks, for as I was once taught, "If you removed the rocks, the brook would lose its song."

Look for the river in every rock. Nothing is wasted in God.

# August 4ᵗʰ
## Easy Way

"If you are the Son of God, command this stone that it be made bread." (Luke 4:3)

Satan's way is always the "easy way." "Well, if you're a Christian, ask God to take away this hard circumstance." Not so the way of God's Warriors. Although we pray so, our hearts should be set: "We know God is able to deliver us out of this...but if not, we will not be moved." The Warrior faces down the rock for what it is: A hard, painful thing. And then rather than begging for that rock to become something comfortable and soft, they say with Jesus, "Man does not live by bread alone, but by every word that proceeds from the mouth of God." And then he waits for the Word of courage, comfort, and confidence that is greater than any rock. There is a word in the Center of that rock! Wait, listen; it will come. God's Glory comes because He knows greater strength is found, not in changing the rock, but in wringing out of it His Power for your life.

# August 5<sup>th</sup>
# Tried

"Until the time that His Word came; the Word of the Lord tried him." (Psalm 105:19)

This verse is about Joseph. There were many years, and much trouble, between the Word God spoke concerning Joseph's chosen call, and the fulfillment. In between, God's Word tested, tried, and purified Joseph. Without that time in-between, Joseph would have been an immature, ineffective leader. The "gap of years" wasn't punishment, but purification, not to hurt, but to prepare him for unspeakable glory.

The greater the Word, the stronger the call, the more necessary the preparation and purification. Don't despair the process; thank Him, because the longer the delay, the more room He is creating in you for greatness and abundant glory and treasures of His Spirit.

# August 6<sup>th</sup>
# Fire

"...who maketh His ministers a flaming fire." (Psalm 104:4a)

Our God is a consuming fire. That fire consumes in His servants all that is impure, all that is not Him. On the altar of our heart of hearts is an Eternal Flame where He calls us to come and lay to the fire every thing that hinders us, hurts us, holds us. The burning of impure things is the fuel that feeds that Holy Fire until it grows and becomes a wildfire in all our life that consumes all we are.

Then we'll understand the fire that "consumes but does not destroy." We <u>become</u> His fire. I <u>want</u> it to be so. In a dark, evil world, I want to burn with passion and love from Jesus' heart, shining brightly, warming and drawing the cold, lonely prisoners and consuming every landmark and stronghold Satan has put up. Let me be a Wildfire, Lord Jesus!

# August 7<sup>th</sup>
## Not Waiting

"They soon forgot His works; they waited not for His counsel." (Psalm 106:13)

What can be worse than doing nothing for God? Doing many things for God - without God being in them or telling you to do them.

Jesus did what He saw the Father doing. He didn't do what was expected or appeared to be right in men's eyes. He waited for His counsel.

Religious works, more than any other thing, frighten me. Satan may not be able to get me to do one bad thing. But he will be content if he can get me to do ten good things that aren't God's things. God can only bless and anoint His touched work, not the multitude of projects and causes we make up to feel religiously good and busy.

God's will and God's work always start with waiting for His counsel. Wait until He speaks. Don Wilkerson once told me his personal prayer: "God, don't bless what I'm doing. Help me do what you are blessing." That's the best counsel I've heard in years!

# August 8th
# Requests

"And He gave them their request, but sent leanness into their soul." (Psalm 106:15)

It's true, just like prosperity preachers tell you: You get what you ask for; you can have what you want. What they don't tell you is that there is a cost. You can satisfy your carnal, material lusts but every demanded human request will empty your soul.

A Christian can either plead with God to get their way, or plead with Jesus to have His way. To the first, you may very well be released to get your worldly fill. To the second, you get Him who satisfies the righteous with good things, but His way, in His time.

It's a matter of trust. Using God to satisfy yourself means you think you know best. The result is spiritual emptiness and a meaningless life, though you may have every earthly pleasure. That will be your "reward." A trusting heart says, "Take it all, just give me Jesus. Father, give me Your best for my life." And no one who has walked this way has ever been sorry; they are rich with HIS riches; they are full, and satisfied, and free.

# August 9<sup>th</sup>
## Envy

"They envied Moses in the camp, and Aaron the saint of the Lord." (Psalm 106:16)

Don't ever envy another great Warrior's place. Like these Israelites, you see only the miracles, the crowds, the position, the <u>power</u>.

What you don't see is the agony, the preparation, the cost, the suffering, the battles, the weakness, the absolute dependency on Jesus for all they are and do.

What you envy is the fruit, the benefits.

On the underside of each great Warrior's life are nights of painful prayer, continual pouring out, tests of rejection and betrayal, the laying down of every human longing on God's altar so that fruit may abound to God's glory.

There is no shortcut to greatness in God.

You only envy what you see, not the heart behind the Warrior. There is a cost that would shake the envy right out of you.

Warriors are made from brokenhearted servants who first see the needs of a bleeding world without Jesus, then see the cost and say, "Whatever it takes, Jesus, use me."

When God raises them, the envy is burned out of them.

# August 10<sup>th</sup>
## Provoking

"Because they provoked his spirit, so that he spoke unadvisedly with his lips." (Psalm 106:33)

The true test of God's character in us is how we respond to provoking words. The other day I saw a servant of God in conversation with an angry young believer, and the young one's words provoked the servant to angry words himself until it almost built to physical blows. Nothing was resolved. Damage was done. Words can't be easily forgotten.

God is determined to find our "hot buttons," expose our un-Christlike reactions which are provoked by another and evidenced by our spoken reaction. The deeper the stream runs, the less a rock thrown into it will disturb it. A shallow pond even a leaf will disturb.

God, give us the grace to "leave off contention" before it begins. Help us to remember that "a soft answer breaks the bone", and that servants must not strive, but be gentle...and if You must, allow others to provoke all the contention out of us so we may see our need to die to the impulse to defend ourselves, prove points or get our way, until all that comes from our heart says, "Let love continue."

# August 11<sup>th</sup>
## Alone

"They wandered in the wilderness in a solitary way."
(Psalm 107:4)

There are times in our walk with God that we walk alone through a difficult thing. Most of the time, God allows the words and support of others to help us through, but there is a time when Jesus wants to be the only One we meet there. You'll know; God will make others unavailable. The words which normally comfort will be empty and even annoying and unhelpful. God is calling. Look for no human help if God has removed that help for a time. Cry out in that dry valley for Him whom your soul loves. There is a depth of relationship He is bringing you to that He could not have when you were surrounded by others. Find Him in that lonely wilderness. When you leave, you'll know in a way nothing will ever change that you will never be alone again.

# August 12<sup>th</sup>
## Rejection

"For my love they are my adversaries: but I give myself unto prayer." (Psalm 108:4)

If you walk with Jesus, you will experience opposition and attack. Paul said <u>all</u> who live godly in Christ <u>shall</u> suffer persecution. There are no exceptions.

Even more painful than the arrows of unbelievers will be misunderstanding and rejection from some believers, even close friends.

What is the only godly response? Not self-pity; not gossip; not strife; not retaliation; not isolation. "I gave myself unto prayer." Jesus didn't specify: "Love your nonchristian enemies; pray for unbelievers who spitefully use you." In fact, it is easier to pray for unbelievers since "they don't know any better." The real test of love is to pray for the unsanctified hurtful Christians who DO know better! If you're wounded by another, then, take it to the Cross; leave it there - a thousand times, if you must - but make no issue of it before the offenders or their friends. You are walking the way of One who knows what it is like and in His triumph, you will triumph too.

# August 13<sup>th</sup>
## Pilgrims

"Thy statutes have been my songs in the house of my pilgrimage." (Psalm 119:54)

The world is becoming more unstable, more dangerous and more destructive by the day. Is it possible to stay strong, even to rejoice in its midst? Yes! If our trust is not in this world system and worldly security, yes! "All things pass. God never changes." If we accept that we are pilgrims, yes! The house of our pilgrimage is our Shelter - the knowledge that wherever we go, He is - whatever happens, He remains. We are pilgrims whose only security is His Presence, His love, and His unchanging Word. That Word is my stability, my strength, my song. I will not cling to changing things and uncertain human securities. I will cling to His unfailing Word, and while I await the end of my pilgrimage, I will sing loudly while I dance through the minefield of life!

# August 14th
# Strong Arm

"O Lord, be gracious unto us; we have waited for thee; be thou their arm every morning..." (Isaiah 33:2)

I've had one of those mornings. You've had them, too - you stub your toe on the wall - drop a carton of milk - pour coffee grounds into the water part of the coffee maker instead of the filter. There are days every muscle hurts from exhaustion, every emotion is empty, and every encouragement has failed. How do I face such a day? I thank You, Father, that You are my Arm every morning - my strong Arm that lets me know You will get me through if I just lean on Your Arm. Your yoke is easy. Your burden is light. Take MY burden, then, Jesus - it is heavy and hard. Free my hand to grasp Your arm. Carry me and lead me through this day, and tomorrow, Your Arm will still be there.

# August 15<sup>th</sup>
# Explained

"But when He was alone with His disciples, He explained everything." (Mark 4:34b)

"Why, God? Why did that happen? Why am I not succeeding? Why do people misunderstand me?"

You can add to this list your own gnawing questions. We all have them.

Most of us, however, throw them down like quick complaints at Father's feet: "Why not?!?" and we rush out of His room to busy ourselves with other matters.

SO MUCH He would explain! But do we take the time to listen? He only speaks when we are still enough to listen. If it's important enough to ask the hard questions, let it be important enough to wait for His reply.

And often, as you do, you'll find, if not answers, or not the answers we expect, the precious Presence of love and security that speaks the answer we most need. "You can trust My love. I will not fail or forsake you." It will be better than the best answer we sought.

# August 16<sup>th</sup>
# Words

"Who has helped you utter these words? And whose spirit spoke from your mouth?" (Job 26:4)

Job was speaking to men who were absolutely convinced of their own rightness. To them, there was no doubt. They were God's spokespeople doing God's will. How dare Job question their motives, their heart? But he did, and it drove them to deeper anger and even surer self-rightness. Their pride made them blind. They never even thought to examine their own hearts.

Yet it is this question - and that ability to look at our heart - that makes us truly His people - if only, before uttering a word, we would stop and ask ourselves, "Where is this coming from? What spirit is about to speak these words?" We could prevent a lot of hurt and learn wisdom from self-restraint and silence. Let no word utter forth from you until you know His Spirit, not yours, has caused you to speak.

# August 17<sup>th</sup>
## Flattery

"For he flattereth himself in his own eyes, until his iniquity be found to be hateful." (Psalm 36:2)

Pride is a wicked thing. Of all the sins, if there were a more damning one, this reigns as king. "The pride of your heart hath deceived thee." (Obadiah 3) Pride is a warped mirror. It takes created, feeble flesh and makes it look exalted and superior when it is nothing more than frail dust. This mirror is deceptive. It takes even godly gifts and makes them appear to be grand titles for our own ego; worse, it makes us believe we are more spiritual and deserving than others. This more than any trap has been the ruin of most leaders of God. A "special revelation" - a ministry "as important as Paul's." Soon we begin pitying and being impatient with those we see as not as "spiritual" as us. Soon that pride is found to be hateful to others. Do you think you are something? What do you have that you haven't been given? And as quick as it was given - it can be taken away. Break the mirror of self-flattery. Of all prayers, the one asking God to destroy our pride seems the most essential.

# August 18<sup>th</sup>
# Human Weapons

"For I will not trust in my bow; neither shall my sword save me." (Psalm 44:6)

Human devices. Even in spiritual matters, obedience often is forsaken for formulas and human weapons. We have a great desire to be in control of all things. "God has to do it this way." "If you do X, then X will happen." The enemy delights in our reducing God to a formula, a set of equations. For he knows that only in surrender to the mind of Christ and complete sensitivity and yielding to His ways is God's will done through us. The prophets had no formula and relied on no human weapons. Human wisdom would say, "Don't do that. It's not common sense." Common sense is God's enemy when it is exalted above obedience! God said, "Go, Ezekiel, lie on your side..." "Go, Jeremiah, put your undergarments inside a wall..." Don't trust the human bow of human thoughts or the sword of human "common sense" formulas. God is wild. He will not be reduced to a formula. His salvation, His will, and His purposes are only fulfilled by those who lay down their carnal weapons and say, "Whatever You ask, I will obey."

# August 19th
## Death

"For this God is our God for ever and ever; He will be our guide even unto death." (Psalm 48:14)

The world faces the subject of death by denying it, delaying it, ignoring it. We don't have that option. God's Word speaks as surely of death as of life; its certainty, its seriousness, its suddenness. Like David, we should ask to be taught to "number our days", to "redeem the time." But even though we know that death is only the door to Jesus' eternal home, we are afraid, aren't we? What is it like? Will I really make it in? What if I am not ready? Will I miss earth and my loved ones there?

While I'm very sure God wants us to live ready, I know He doesn't want us to live in fear of that moment. I am just as certain that it is useless to worry about death. "But I'm afraid. I'm not strong! What if it's sudden? A long death? A painful one?" Dear one, hasn't God been sufficient thus far in everything? Hasn't He given you grace for every need? Has He ever left you comfortless? And didn't He say not to be concerned over tomorrow's troubles? Isn't grace always there <u>when you need it</u> - not before? Be at peace - when death comes, grace will break forth to carry you in joy to new life! He will be your Guide - even in death! Trust Him, even in death - it will have no victory over you!

# August 20<sup>th</sup>
## Daily Prayers

"Evening, and morning, and at noon, I will pray, and cry aloud; and He shall hear My voice." (Psalm 55:17)

Paul told us to pray without ceasing. This verse gives an outline, a framework for daily prayer. God gave three parts to each day. At each station is a different perspective, there are different challenges and different problems. When we say a hasty prayer in the morning rush or just a sleepy "goodnight" prayer (who ever really finishes those pillow prayers before Mr. Sandman knocks us out?) we simply acknowledge God's Presence. That's good, but not very helpful to *us*. Help comes when we take these three times in the day to bring our problems to Him, discuss our concerns, and thank Him for His help and His answers. In the quiet before the morning traffic hums, we set God before us as the Master of our Day. At noon we ask His help and guidance and strength in the midst of what we brought before Him earlier. And at night, we reflect, see what we've learned and what He has done, which encourages us to face tomorrow. It is much like a child who shares their school day with a loving parent at home. For me, that was the best part of my childhood, knowing love always waited for me at home, eager to say, "What did you do today? What did you learn? How was your day?" It's like that with Father. It is one of the sweetest comforts I know and turns daily prayers into loving communion and sharing.

# August 21st
# A Wonder

"I am as a wonder to many; but You are my strong refuge." (Psalm 71:7)

If you really, truly set your heart to follow Jesus, you too will be a "wonder to many". People will scratch their heads over you. "What's with them, anyway?" Old friends, even family may become strangers to you because they can't understand your singular devotion to One Unseen. Following Jesus means "common sense" takes a back seat to obedience, and obedience creates concern in others that "you've taken this God thing too far this time." But you will live in a world where popular approval and "being liked" ceases (although slowly and painfully) to matter. Obedience to Another Call leaves many "wondering" about you. They can't figure you out! A true Warrior will always be an enigma; they seem to move and live in a world cross-grained to all this world holds dear, though they touch that world deeper and effect it stronger than its half-dead residents. Sometimes this difference and rejection hurts. Know that Jesus is your strong refuge where you can find acceptance and courage to live in obedience no matter what others do.

# August 22nd
# Appearance

"As He was praying, the appearance of His face changed..." (Luke 9:29a)

There is useless, vain, self-serving prayer, like the Pharisee saying, "I'm thankful I'm not like others," or those Jesus said thought they would be heard because of their repetitious prayers. And we all know - or maybe have <u>been</u> - those who "pray at" people while praying in prayer groups - using prayer to "preach" at others we think need to hear what we pray. It's all useless.

How do we know real prayer? It "changes our face". Our heart is softer, our actions more like Jesus, our steps filled with faith in Him and our words and lives filled with Jesus' love. True prayer makes a difference in how we talk, think, live and look. It transforms - not because it's a "tool" or a "method" - but because in intimate relationship with Jesus through prayer, we touch God, and as a torch touched to a fire, we cannot keep from being lit afire.

# August 23<sup>rd</sup>
## Trust

"Revive us to trust in You." (Psalm 80:18)

O Lord, hear our prayer. The years have passed, and with it, our lives have begun to fade to gray amidst the trouble, turmoil and ordinary tasks of daily living. How well we were warned by Jesus that the cares of this world would choke the living Word, and how we feel the choking. O Father, our hearts so often grow tired and dull, busy and uncaring.

And yet, we remember the first days, when all that mattered was Jesus, when all we longed for was Your Word, Your Presence and Your Love. Revive us, Lord, to trust in You again. O Lord, we ask for revival, but so often we wait for an external visit by Your Spirit somewhere, in a building, in a church, far away or near. But we need revival the moment we wake in the morning, before the pulling and the tugging of this world overwhelm us and put You in the background of our hearts.

Revive us, O Lord. We need Your touch once more.

# August 24<sup>th</sup>
# Bitter Things

"The full soul loatheth an honeycomb; but to the hungry soul every bitter thing is sweet." Proverbs 27:7

You can tell a lot by looking at people's faces. And I find those who have the most, tend to be the most arrogant, the most greedy, the most unhappy. They are ungrateful for even the smallest gifts they have received.

It has been such a contrast over the years to see and walk with those Christians who have had so little, and who have had such suffering. Even the smallest thing they have is received with great grace and gratefulness.

The real key here is the last part of the verse: "To the hungry soul, every bitter thing is sweet." Hungry for God, they have learned that even what is bitter in life has the sweetness of His higher plan and deepening love. Isn't that better than all the pleasures of the world?

# August 25th
# Joy

"For God has given us these times of joy; they are scheduled in the laws of Israel." (Psalm 81:4)

Life is undeniably full of pain and trial. Some experience it more than others. But we have to know that that is only part of our walk with Him. There is much value in learning how to rejoice in even the worst of times and circumstances.

Beyond that - I have come to realize God has something even more wonderful. The Hebrews actually had celebrations of joy in their LAW - it wasn't optional! How much more does God want us to enjoy the great and simple blessings of the everyday - to revel in a sunset - to laugh with your kids until you hurt - to savor a cup of coffee - to drink in every lovely gift in every day. We are too bound. We are too joyless. We are too afraid. May God schedule times of joy in our lives - overwhelming, hilarious joy. What good Father does not absolutely delight in the laughter and unrestrained joy of his own children?

# August 26<sup>th</sup>
# Respond

"For God so loved the world that He gave his only begotten son, that whosoever believes on Him should not perish but have everlasting life." – John 3:16

At a time when the world seems filled with hatred toward those that love God and serve Jesus, and they oppose all that is righteous and good, we cannot afford to act as they do and respond in kind. God still loves the world. And even in the face of total opposition and rejection, we must be vessels of His love, or there is no hope to reach the lost. It's not compromise. It's the cure. Paul's salvation came after witnessing the undeserved forgiveness while stoning Stephen to death.

Respond – don't react. Without salvation, the unsaved can do no more than what they are already doing. God's love leads to the cross, forgiveness, and redemption.

# August 27th

## Point To The Light

"He was not that Light, but was sent to bear witness of that light." - John 1:8

In an age of Facebook followers and celebrity everything, those of us who bear his Word to the world and the church need to make sure we are always putting the spotlight on the Light of the world – Jesus.

Human sinful nature always seeks to be in the spotlight, and follow those in the spotlight. Paul himself was no stranger to this dilemma:

"Who then is Paul, and who is Apollos, but ministers by whom you believed, even as the Lord gave to every man? I have planted, Apollos watered; but God gave the increase. So then neither is he that plants any thing, neither he that waters; but God that giveth the increase." (1 Corinthians 3:5-7)

Church leaders were never meant to be in a popularity contest.

God keep us humble, seek to follow You and always point to Your light.

# August 28<sup>th</sup>

# Shields Up

"And when the devil had ended all the temptation, he departed from Him for a season." – Luke 4:13.

Nehemiah's builders always worked with one hand and had a sword in the other.

The devil is relentless. If he leaves us alone, it is only for a season, always looking for a way to take us out of the battle. The biggest mistake we make is to lay down our armor thinking we can slide. If he departs for a season, be ready for him with the sword when he returns. Shields up!

# August 29ᵗʰ

## Fire

"He shall baptize you with the Holy Spirit and with fire." Luke 3:16b

Jesus does miracles. He does fill us with his Holy Spirit and graces us with life-changing touches, healings, and deliverance.

However, many of us seek a supernatural experience but shrink back from the baptism of fire. When he baptizes us with fire - with confrontation, cleansing, and difficult trials and painful circumstances surround us, we are overwhelmed and wonder if these things mean that God has left us. It is quite the opposite. His love is a fire that is determined to cleanse us of everything that is not Him. He is as near in the fire of trials as he is in the blessings and miracles. He will use every difficult thing if you let Him, to make you more like Jesus.

"But He knows the way that I take: when He has tried me, I shall come forth as gold." – Job 23:10

# August 30$^{th}$

# God in the Wilderness

"...the Word of God came unto John the son of Zacharias in the wilderness." Luke 3:2

Whatever your personal wilderness is, God will meet you there. The Bible is full of places of crisis and wilderness where God met, changed and blessed his people – Joseph in prison being prepared to lead a nation, Jacob in fear when he wrestled with the angel and was given a new name, Jesus being tempted in the wilderness and returning from that wilderness in the power of the Holy Spirit, John in exile and given The Revelation.

In your crisis or wilderness, a simple prayer: "Jesus, meet me here." His Word will come to you where you are, and you will come up out of the wilderness "leaning on your Beloved." (Song of Solomon 8:5)

Let your crisis place be His meeting place.

# August 31st

## Edit Buttons

"But Mary kept all these things, and pondered them in her heart." Luke 2:19

We live in an age where our "edit button" is broken, and we are encouraged to just blurt out – or post – whatever comes to our mind or our mouth.

Mary gives us a godly role model here. Before we say, post, text or tweet, think it thoroughly through. Words have consequences, always. Once words are written or spoken, they cannot be retrieved.

An old building expression applies here too: Measure twice, cut once. Do that with your words as well. And always ask yourself: is it true? Is it helpful? Is it the godly thing to do or say?

Following Mary's example here will keep you from a world of hurt.

# September 1<sup>st</sup>

## Direction

"To give light to them that sit in darkness and in the shadow of death, to guide our feet into the way of peace." Luke 1:79

"Seek peace and pursue it." 1 Peter 3:11

How do you know God's direction? How do you know what he wants you to do? Follow after peace. Not an emotional feeling which can easily be changed by fear or circumstances, but the "peace that passes all understanding."

There will be times when circumstances seem to oppose the direction you feel God is leading you, and yet you feel that peace of God to pursue that direction. At other times, the way will seem completely clear and the choice seems to make sense, and yet you have an unease about moving in that direction. Follow after peace.

Get time with the Lord to listen. Let that peace that passes all understanding guide your feet into the way of peace in the direction He wants you to go.

# September 2<sup>nd</sup>
## True Discipleship

"To make ready a people prepared for the Lord."
- Luke 1:17b

This is the simple plan of discipleship. How do we do this? Word, worship, fellowship and prayer.

To the extent that we invest in these three things in our churches, we are making disciples. Whatever distracts from this or complicates it, defeats the heart of true discipleship.

The challenge is to take all of our programs, plans, activities, and busywork and to ask God to help us to rid ourselves of anything that takes away from those simple and crucial disciple-making tools.

# September 3rd

## Unchanging Love

"Then Jesus beholding him loved him, and said to him, one thing you lack: go your way, sell whatever you have, and give to the poor, and you shall have treasure in heaven: and come, take up the cross, and follow me. " Mark 10:21

Jesus looked at him, and loved him. I was deeply touched by this. Jesus knew he was not going to follow him. And yet, he looked at him, and loved him.

I think sometimes when we sin or fail we picture Jesus looking at us with anger or disgust. But even though we fail him, even though we sin against Him, He looks at us, and He loves us. I can't fathom that kind of love. It is a love that even this moment reduces me to tears. It is a love that makes me want to not fail, to not sin. "Herein is love, not that we loved God, but that he loved us, and sent His Son to be the propitiation for our sins. (1 John 4:10)

Thank You, Jesus, for your unchanging love to this undeserving son!

# September 4ᵗʰ

## Unbelief

"And straightway The father of the child cried out, and said with tears, Lord, I believe; help my unbelief!" Mark 9:24

Sometimes the struggles are so great that we find it hard to hang on. This verse has been a great comfort in times when all my heart wants to trust Jesus, but fear and doubt seek to rob me of faith. Lord, I believe – please help my unbelief! And he strengthens my faith, as he will yours. "For He knows our frame; He remembers that we are dust." (Psalm 103:14) At times faith is not the absence of doubt but the proclamation of faith regardless of the doubt. And our compassionate Father will help us in all our weakness to be people of faith in the midst of all our trials.

# September 5th

## Healing Ways

"And He took the blind man by the hand, and led him out of the town; and when He had spit on his eyes, He asked him if he saw anything. And he looked up and said, I see men as trees, walking. After that He put his hands again upon his eyes, and made him look up: and he was restored and saw every man clearly." Mark 8:23-25

God heals in different ways. Sometimes it's not all at once. When we struggle with heart wounds or besetting sins, we can feel defeated because we aren't healed or delivered right away. But some wounds are deep, and some healings require more than one work of Jesus, much as some surgeries require more than one operation. But be sure of this: Jesus will not relent until your healing and deliverance are complete. Don't give up.

# September 6<sup>th</sup>

## Scorn

"And they laughed Him to scorn." Mark 5:40

Matthew, Mark, and Luke all record this account of the crowds laughing at Jesus before he raised a little girl from the dead.

The world will always laugh at The gospel and make fun of Jesus. Don't be offended if they do the same to you. Thank God that you are worthy to be counted in the same company as your Master.

It reminds me of the words of an old Keith Green song:

So many laughing at Jesus,
Well, the funniest thing that he's done
Is love this old stubborn, rebellious world while their hate for him just goes on

We must love people as well even though they laugh at what they do not understand. "Father forgive them; they don't know what they're doing."

# September 7<sup>th</sup>

## Forgiveness

"When Jesus saw their faith he said unto the sick of the palsy, thy sins be forgiven thee." Mark 2:5

Our need to be forgiven is greater than any need we have. Nothing - not illness, not financial need, not loneliness nor fear - needs God's touch more than our need for forgiveness. If we know that we are forgiven and have eternal life, then no matter what else, we can say, "it is well with my soul."

# September 8<sup>th</sup>

## Moved With Compassion

"And Jesus, moved with compassion, put forth his hand and touched him, and said to him, 'I will. Be healed.' " Mark 1:41

God deliver me from sterile religious works of have-to's and shoulds. Help me have the heart of Jesus that is moved with compassion for others, and seeks to bring your mercy, forgiveness, grace, and healing to others – not because I should, but because your love compels me and moves my heart with your compassion.

# September 9th

## Destroyer

"But the chief priests and elders persuaded the multitude that they should ask for Barabbas, and destroy Jesus." Mt. 27:20.

Now the full nature and motive of Satan is exposed. He is a destroyer. He wants to destroy Jesus. Not hurt him, not discourage him, but utterly annihilate him.

Have no doubt - he wants to do the same to you. He cannot hurt God's heart unless he is able to hurt you. And make no mistake about it, he's not out to just hurt you, but to completely destroy you. That is what he does. That is who he is.

Take the battle against him as seriously as he takes the battle against you and allow him not one tiny inch of room in your life. He comes to kill, steal and destroy. Jesus came to give you life and life more abundantly.

Nurture and grow all that speaks of that Life of Jesus, and rid yourself of every bit of leaven from the destroyer.

# September 10<sup>th</sup>

## Bitter

"And Peter remembered the word of Jesus who had said to him, 'Before the rooster crows, you will deny Me three times.' So he went out and wept bitterly." Matthew 26:75

There will be in our walk moments of bitter weeping.

In Exodus 15:22-25, there were bitter waters, but God showed Moses a tree which when thrown in the waters, made them sweet.

The cross is the tree God placed in our bitter waters which will make them sweet. He has borne our griefs. He carries our sorrows. You do not weep alone. He will turn your mourning into dancing, and dry every tear.

# September 11<sup>th</sup>
## Deception

"Take heed that no one deceives you." Matthew 24:4

This was for believers. This is for you and me.

How do you guard against getting deceived as so many are today?

1. Know the word of God deeply.

2. Know the God of the Word intimately.

3. Have some good friends or family who will knock you upside the head if they see you getting weird.

And ask Jesus daily to keep you from all deception.

# September 12ᵗʰ

## Transparency

"Even so you also outwardly appear righteous to men, but within you are full of hypocrisy and iniquity." Matthew 23:28.

It is my heart's desire to be the same person inside and out. It takes a lifetime. I don't want to be a different person around others than I am when I am alone. Transparency is scary, but it's a real goal. I believe when we can be transparent with a few people we trust and say, "This is who I am, and I need Jesus to help me be more like Him," then we start to become real Christians. God deliver us from hypocrisy - the "hiding behind the mask." Deliver us from spiritual play-acting. Every day I am still in need of a Savior.

# September 13<sup>th</sup>

## Walking in the Word

"Jesus answered and said to them, 'you are mistaken, not knowing the Scriptures, nor the power of God.' " (Matthew 22:29)

There are those who know a few scriptures but wield them like a club and do not believe in the power of His Word to heal, deliver and set free today. There are others who believe in God's power but do not have the discernment that comes from the Word of God to know the difference between a work of God and a counterfeit supernatural manifestation. We must have a strong knowledge of the word of God as well as a solid walk in the power of our God that still does miracles today. Jesus, help us to know your Word well and walk in your power every day. Help us not to batter people with your Word nor let people fall into error by ignoring it.

# September 14<sup>th</sup>

## Surrender

And whosoever shall fall on this stone shall be broken: but whoever it falls on, it will grind him to powder." Matthew 8:44.

God is determined to make us more like Jesus. We can do that the hard way or the easy way. Choose to be broken before God and let Him fill us and change us, or resist Him and be shattered because our pride wanted to do things our way. 40 days or 40 years in the wilderness? Trust me, 40 days is much better!

# September 15<sup>th</sup>

## Not Menpleasers

"Then came His disciples, and said to Him, 'Do you know that the Pharisees were offended after they heard this saying?'" Matthew 15:12)

In this Captain Obvious moment, the disciples were concerned that Jesus didn't seem to be aware that He offended the Pharisees. Of course he was aware! He simply didn't care. His objective was not to please anyone, but to please the Father. As His disciples, we should never take a poll before we tell the truth to see if people are going to be upset by it, or whether it will cost us friends or finances. We need to speak the truth in love, (and you better make sure it's in love and not just coming from your flesh!) and leave the rest to God. "Woe unto you, when all men shall speak well of you! for so did their fathers to the false prophets." (Luke 6:26)

Popularity is not always a good thing.

# September 16th

## Offenses

Matthew 18:15 "Moreover if your brother sins against you, go and tell him his fault between you and him alone. If he hears you, you have gained your brother."

How much grief, how much pain would be avoided if we followed this simple command. Instead of going to each other, we go to others about each other creating pockets of gossip and widening the divide. Following this command is not easy, but the damage done in churches by not following it is incalculable. Do the hard thing. Is there someone you need to reconcile with? To forgive? To ask forgiveness from? Don't delay. Do it today.

# September 17th

# The Cross

"If any man will come after me, let him deny himself, and take up his cross, and follow Me." (Matthew 17:23-24)

I confess that this is almost foreign to me. I think it is to most of us. I am concerned with being inconvenienced, not with serving. I am concerned with my rights, not my calling as a servant. I have not attained, and I am convicted this morning at how little I really live this.

The cross was a humiliation. My flesh would rather prove my point; my pride would rather have me be angry and adversarial rather than humble and grateful for even the little things.

Pride - the opposite of a servant's heart - is the killer of true serving and the source of most of our failure to love and reconcile with each other.

One of the things I loved about the youth I was blessed to serve in the last several years was our common greeting, "You're better than me. " "No, you're better than me." It was the truth God taught me from Philippians 2:3 - "Let nothing be done through strife or vainglory; but in lowliness of mind let each esteem other better than themselves." (Many of you are still living this out. I am so proud of you!)

The need for true serving and true humbleness among believers has never been greater. Jesus, help us - help ME - take up that cross.

# September 18<sup>th</sup>

## Leaven

"Your glorying is not good. Do you not know that a little leaven leavens the whole lump? Therefore purge out the old leaven, that you may be a new lump, since you truly are unleavened. For indeed Christ, our Passover, was sacrificed for us. Therefore let us keep the feast, not with old leaven, nor with the leaven of malice and wickedness, but with the unleavened bread of sincerity and truth." 1 Corinthians 5:6-8

This is a time of purging all the "leaven" out of our lives. What is leaven? It is a germ that grows and has the ability to affect and change everything. It is yeast that transforms bread and makes it grow.

Sin is the leaven. Jesus forgave it, but we've got to get rid of it. What hinders you? What "besetting sin" keeps you from a full walk? It could be outward things: habits, addictions, things you own you know you need to get rid of, things you view that you know are evil. it could be heart things: bitterness, anger, unforgiveness, pride, pettiness or stinginess.

Ask God in this time to put His finger on even the tiniest leaven and remove it from your life. Do you feel helpless to give it up, or change your heart? "Not by power, nor by might, but by My Spirit, say the Lord of hosts." He will help you. He can deliver you from even the toughest bondage, the hardest heart-sin.

May God help us all to sweep our hearts from every germ of sin.

# September 19<sup>th</sup>

## Grace Through the Cross

"It is of little use to cry with Jabez, 'oh that that thou wouldst bless me indeed,' unless, like him, we ask, 'keep me from evil.'" (FB Meyer)

"Create in me a clean heart, O God." Psalm 51:10.

As believers, we all sin. We all need cleansing. And God's blessing always follows repentance, brokenness, heart-searching, honest confession and cleansing at the Cross.

Today's "new church" message is blessing without brokenness. A pulpit message that does not pierce the heart has no power to change it.

His grace is always at the foot of the cross.

# September 20<sup>th</sup>

## Jesus on the Throne

"He must increase, but I must decrease." John 3:30

As children, it is expected that they crave attention and are the center of their world. As they mature, their world should become less about them and more about others. Our culture, however, teaches that YOU are the most important person in your life, and it is about your needs, your way, your rights.

Thank God for Jesus who takes the center, takes us off of our throne and places Himself there. We no longer need to be the center of things. Our needs take a backseat to the needs of others and the will of the Father.

A sure sign of maturity is that it is no longer about what God can do for us and how others can serve us, but about how we can serve others and Jesus can be seen, even if we stay in the shadows. God grant us the grace to decrease so that you might increase through us.

# September 21$^{st}$

## Cleansed

"For if ye forgive men their trespasses, your heavenly Father will also forgive you." Matthew 6:14

I love the story I heard about the little kid in Sunday School who mis-recited this part of the Lord's prayer: "Forgive us our trash passes as we forgive those who pass trash against us."

What a simple and awesome message. People will always try to pass trash about you and to you about others. Ignore it, forgive it. And stop passing trash about other people. God, keep our hearts clean from trash!

# September 22$^{nd}$

## Finishing Grace

"But by the grace of God I am what I am." 1 Corinthians 15:10.

My past doesn't determine what I am. God's grace does. Neither what others think of me, nor what I think of myself, matters. If God has set His love on me and determined to use me for His kingdom, then the opinion of all the hordes of hell matter to me not one bit.

Thank God that He put you where you are, made you who you are, and will use you for His glory as you are while making you into His image.

We are all works in progress; as the old man said, "I'm not who I want to be, and I'm not who I'm going to be, but thank God, I'm not who I used to be." And at this moment, by his grace, I am what I am.

And He is not finished with me yet!

"Beloved, now are we the sons of God, and it does not yet appear what we shall be: but we know that, when he shall appear, we shall be like him; for we shall see him as he is." 1 John 3:2

# September 23rd

## Unequally Yoked

"Be ye not unequally yoked together with unbelievers."
2 Corinthians 6:14b

So many youth lose their walk by convincing themselves that the boy/girl they are falling for is a "Christian" - when in fact that person is just playing the God-card just to get what they want - then find out they'd been deceived.

# September 24<sup>th</sup>

## Warfare Not Optional

"The thief cometh not, but for to steal, and to kill, and to destroy: I am come that they might have life, and that they might have it more abundantly." John 10:10

When the world is faced with an incomprehensible evil act, they want to blame mental illness, because it "explains" an evil act that seems to have no motive. (Even when no evidence of mental illness existed.) People are afraid to face the possibility that evil and evil spirits exist and are capable of taking over people and doing incomprehensible evil acts. Spiritual warfare is not optional for believers. Prayer is powerful. Repentance is the call of the hour. Just my prayerful thoughts.

# September 25<sup>th</sup>

## Prophecy

"Knowing this first, that there shall come in the last days scoffers..."

"Yeah, well people have been talking about the last days and Jesus coming back for centuries."

"Knowing this first, that there shall come in the last days scoffers, walking after their own lusts, And saying, Where is the promise of his coming? for since the fathers fell asleep, all things continue as they were from the beginning of the creation." 2 Peter 3:3-4

I have a feeling there are going to be a lot of people very regretful they did not teach their people about biblical prophecy concerning the days we are in. I am so grateful for Pastor Rick Howard for never wavering in teaching the truth on these matters.

"When you see these things begin to come to pass, look up and lift your heads, for your redemption draws nigh." (Luke 21:28)

# September 26th

## Watch Your Words

"Let your speech be always with grace, seasoned with salt, that ye may know how ye ought to answer every man." Colossians 4:6

There is a time to speak out against lies, and we must do so when required. But you can speak the truth in love without resorting to fleshly, sarcastic and ugly attacks.

And never, ever use the words idiot, retard, or other invectives if you claim the Name of Jesus.

We can speak truth without humiliating and mocking other people.

Always, ALWAYS make sure you have ALL the facts straight before allowing your emotions to drive your postings.

# September 27<sup>th</sup>

## Gossip

"Where no wood is, there the fire goes out. So where there is no talebearer the strife ceases." Proverbs 27:20

The best way to stop gossip is to stop feeding it. Starve a gossip of their audience and they will go away.

# September 28<sup>th</sup>

## Spare Your Words

"He that hath knowledge spareth his words: and a man of understanding is of an excellent spirit." - Proverbs 17:27

Sometimes a tweet-length bit of godly counsel does more good than a sermon-length piece of advice.

# September 29<sup>th</sup>

## Restraint

"The beginning of strife is as when one letteth out water: therefore leave off contention, before it be meddled with." - Proverbs 17:14

When you feel the adrenaline that comes with being about to enter into a huge argument, just excuse yourself and walk away. You will save yourself a lot of grief, and a lot of words you wished you would have never said that you can never take back. Keep the floodgate closed.

# September 30<sup>th</sup>

## Tried

"The fining pot is for silver, and the furnace for gold: but the LORD trieth the hearts. " -Proverbs 17:3

Heated circumstances are God's tools to cleanse, change and refine us to be more like Jesus. It is evidence of his work in our life. Only be concerned when things are going too smoothly for too long. (My suspicion is that most of my Christian friends don't know that "smooth sailing" experience!)

# October 1<sup>st</sup>

## Searching

"All the ways of a man are clean in his own eyes; but the Lord weighs the spirits." Proverbs 16:2.

The fact that my first instinct is always to defend my own position or argument and lash out at the other person proves this scripture to be true. My default (and fleshly) position is to always assume my own rightness of heart. But God knows the truth, and I should always go to the Lord and ask Him to show me my heart and rid me of the terrible junk I have in there. (And we all do.) Our default position in personal conflict with others should always first be, "Is it me, Lord?" "Create in me a clean heart, O Lord..."

# October 2nd

## Do You Love Me?

"So when they had dined, Jesus said to Simon Peter, Simon, son of Jonas, do you love Me more than these?" - John 21:15

Few questions in the scriptures are more searching or more personal. "Do you love Me more than these?" More than cars, houses, jobs, position? More than friends, loved ones, family? More than this life and all its pleasures? More than your dearest love, your nearest friend?

"Lord, you know I do," Peter replied. I want Peter's reply to be my reply. In my weakness, Jesus, help me love You more than them all.

# October 3rd

## Relationship

"Come and eat." (John 21:12)

John 21 is one of the most touching chapters in scripture to me. Jesus had already risen from the dead. His disciples still didn't know what to do with it all, and Peter was back to fishing. Jesus calls out from the shore to ask if they had caught anything. They said no. He told them to cast their nets out, and suddenly they had more fish that they knew what to do with. They knew it was Jesus. When they came in from the water, Jesus had already cooked breakfast for them. Think about that. God the son, resurrected from the dead, king of the universe… made them breakfast and just wanted to sit and eat with them. He wanted to be with them. Just like he wants to be with you and me. "Come and eat." The world, history, the future and eternity had been changed forever by Jesus's resurrection, but in this moment, he and his disciples came together just to be together, share a meal and be in each other's company.

It's all about relationship with Jesus. He is love is beyond my comprehension.

## October 4<sup>th</sup>

# Kept

"I pray not that You should take them out of the world, but that You should keep them from the evil." - John 17:15

We cannot effectively reach the world if we have isolated ourselves from those who live in it. But we cannot effectively reach them if we are infected by the things of the world. We must be in the world without allowing the world to be in us.

How much of the world is in you? How much of your speech reflects the world and its ways, as opposed to words that are godly and scriptural? Important things to ask ourselves.

# October 5<sup>th</sup>

## Reindeer Friends

" A friend loveth at all times, and there is a friend that sticketh closer than a brother." Proverbs 17:17

Rudolph's friends made fun of him because his nose was red and they cut him out of the herd. But when Rudolph saved the day, suddenly "all of the reindeer loved him."

Rudolph needs to get rid of his fair-weather reindeer friends and get some real reindeer buddies who don't care about his nose and will stick with him even if he's not a hero.

Christmas thoughts in 100-degree fall weather...

# October 6<sup>th</sup>

## Pruning

Jesus said that every branch that bears fruit, he prunes so it can bear more fruit. (John 15:2) One meaning is that He prunes the "useless shoots." We call them "runners," shoots that take up water and soil but are completely fruitless.

Lord, cut away the useless shoots in our lives: the time-wasting activities, the ungodly relationships, and every and any thing that will make us spiritually barren and rob us of the life-giving power of Your Spirit. Spare no shoot. Prune relentlessly- and constantly. Make us a fruitful tree.

# October 7<sup>th</sup>

## Fruit

"For every tree is known by his own fruit. For of thorns men do not gather figs, nor of a bramble bush gather they grapes." Luke 6:44

Mini-revelation: Out in the garden today, I noticed that I have massive climbing vines that are supposed to grow snow peas. But that's all I have, vines. It's not bearing fruit.

I realized that we can have a big church or ministry and lots of "growth" in numbers and activities, but if it is not bearing FRUIT it is nothing more than decoration.

Are our churches and ministries bearing fruit for the Kingdom? Or are we just a wild vine that won't stop expanding? Hard questions worth asking in our "success oriented ministry" times!

# October 8<sup>th</sup>

# Stay Under

"You therefore endure hardness, as a good soldier of Jesus Christ." – 2 Timothy 2:3

It is in our human nature to want to escape hardship and suffering, circumstances, or a person who is causing us pain or difficulty. But so often the word of scriptures is to "endure." One of the words for endure often used is, "hypomeno" which means to stand under. A similar word means to stand and carry on our shoulders. I have come to know that running is easier; attempting to change location or circumstances to avoid difficulty is our first response. But many times God's word is to stay under those things until He changes them, knowing that it is those very circumstances that are transforming you and making of you a true and prepared soldier of the Lord Jesus Christ, ready for any battle that may come. My prayer is that those who are suffering under difficulties right now will find comfort in these words, knowing that God knows where you are, what you are going through, and He will use every single difficulty to fit you for His kingdom work, and for eternal blessings beyond your fondest dreams.

# October 9th

## Hated for Truth

"The world cannot hate you, but Me it hates, because I testify of it, that the works thereof are evil." -John 7:7

"And you shall be hated of all men for my name's sake." - Luke 21:17

We must never lose our commission to speak truth about the evil works in this world, and that the ONLY answer is Jesus. Expect to be hated for it. And never let that fact keep you from speaking it anyway.

# October 10th

## Never

"All that the Father gives Me shall come to me; and him that comes to Me I will in no wise cast out." - John 6:37

Have you struggled and failed and sinned? Have you come to Jesus needing forgiveness but are afraid that you have gone too far, and that He will shut the door of grace in your face? Take comfort! His Word remains true. He will "in no wise" - meaning NEVER - cast you out. In your grief and brokenness over your failure, run like the Prodigal into your loving Savior's arms. Drink deep from the eternal fountain of grace and forgiveness He bought for you with His own blood.

# October 11<sup>th</sup>

## Stay

"So when the Samaritans had come to Him they urged Him to stay with them..." -John 4:40

"But they constrained Him, saying, stay with us..." - Luke 24:29

Stay with us, Jesus, for the day is far spent. Stay with us in the darkness and the light, in the day and in the night. Stay with us when our hearts ache. Stay with us when we feel friendless and alone. Though others may leave us, stay with us. Though everything in life fails us, stay with us. You are all we desire and all we need. Stay with us, Jesus.

And Jesus said, "I am with you always, even to the end of the world."

# October 12th

# Blindness

"He trusted in God; let him deliver him now, if he will have him: for he said, I am the Son of God." Mt. 27:43

"All they do that see me laugh me to scorn: they shoot out the lip, they shake the head, saying, 'he trusted on the Lord that he would deliver him: let him deliver him, seeing he delighted in him.' " Psalm 22:7-8

The first verse was spoken by the Pharisees at Jesus' crucifixion to mock him. The very ones that counted themselves as righteous keepers of the law were actually the mockers spoken of in the Psalms concerning the Messiah. And they were completely blind to it.

I marvel at the absolute accurate perfection of biblical prophecy. And I tremble to think it is possible to count yourself as righteous and yet be blind to the truth.

This Passover, May God deliver us from the leaven of spiritual blindness and self-righteousness. Grant us the gift of humility and self-examination. "Examine yourselves, whether you be in the faith." 1 Cor. 13:5.

# October 13<sup>th</sup>

## Battlefield

"Put on the whole armour of God, that ye may be able to stand against the wiles of the devil." Ephesians 6:11

I posted this before from streams in the desert but this morning it seemed especially important:

"We would better creep away from the battlefield at once if we are not going to be brave."

The Christian life is not a spectator sport. It is a real battle. God make us His brave souls on the battlefield!

# October 14<sup>th</sup>

## Roots

If God were just concerned with our outward sins and ungodly words and actions, the scriptures would have said he was coming to lay the ax to the base of the trees.

Ask Jesus to lay the ax to the root. The rest will die in time.

# October 15<sup>th</sup>

## Discernment

"But strong meat belongeth to them that are of full age, even those who by reason of use have their senses exercised to discern both good and evil." Hebrews 5:14

Our discernment concerning people and church matters can be greatly clouded and even dangerous when seen through the eyes of personal hurt. Lord, give us clear discernment that is free from our personal stake in the outcome.

# October 16<sup>th</sup>

## Resolutions

Resolutions:

"Break up your fallow ground and do not sow among thorns." - Jeremiah 4:3

Where has my heart become hardened - "fallow ground?" In worship? In devotion time? In praying for others?

Where am I sowing among thorns - worthless things? Too many hours with ungodly friends? Too much time on video games? An obsession with politics? Sports? Netflix bingeing? O Lord I cannot redeem those hours once they are gone! Please help me sow into Your Word, Your work and Your presence.

# October 17<sup>th</sup>

## Forgotten

"Yet My people have forgotten Me for days without number."
– Jeremiah 2:32b

I feel the conviction of this, this morning. It's not that I intend to forget God. But it is simply so easy to let days go by and neglect the reading of His word and the sweetness of His presence. There is always so much to do. The days grow shorter. But the truth is, without that time in His presence, I am simply doing busy work. Fruitless, meaningless paper shuffling.

Help me, Jesus, to fight for that time with you. Nothing else will give me the power of Your Spirit to fulfill Your calling.

# October 18<sup>th</sup>

## Swearing

"Let no corrupt communication proceed out of your mouth, but that which is good to the use of edifying, that it may minister grace unto the hearers." Ephesians 4:29

Swearing is a sign of how angry you are.
Swearing is a sign of how insecure you are.
Swearing is not a cultural norm, but a spiritual compromise.

It's not a sign of strength, but weakness.
Out of the abundance of the heart, the mouth speaks.
Not a judgment, just a heart test.

# October 19<sup>th</sup>

## Resolved…

"And whatsoever ye do, do it heartily, as to the Lord, and not unto men;" Colossians 3:23

Walk in joy
Make bold moves
Sing like you don't care how it sounds.
You hide behind the bold line
and barely touch it so you won't have to be
embarrassed or humiliated.
Break that line like a long-distance champion.
God is cheering you on;
that's all the applause you'll ever need.

# October 20<sup>th</sup>

## What God Says

"Say not, 'I am only a youth.'"Jeremiah 1:8

What God says about you is all that matters. Not what others say or think, not what you say or think, and certainly not what the accuser says or thinks. I say this with love: Stop contradicting God and His Word about you. The Bible says you are accepted in the Beloved if you belong to Jesus. (Ephesians 1:6) Believe it. Speak it. By God's grace, live it. "I am all He says I am."

# October 21st

## Beulah Land

I can see far down the mountain,
Where I wandered weary years,
Often hindered in my journey
By the ghosts of doubts and fears;
Broken vows and disappointments
Thickly sprinkled all the way,
But the Spirit led, unerring,
To the land I hold today.

Tell me not of heavy crosses,
Nor of burdens hard to bear,
For I've found this great salvation
Makes each burden light appear;
And I love to follow Jesus,
Gladly counting all but dross,
Worldly honors all forsaking
For the glory of the cross.

- Is This Not the Land of Beulah?
By William Hunter

# October 22<sup>nd</sup>

## The Way

"Pray that the Lord your God may show us the way in which we should walk and the thing that we should do." - Jeremiah 42:3.

There is no point in asking God to show you the way to go if you are not willing to do the thing He has asked you to do to get there. Direction minus obedience equals disobedience.

# October 23rd

## Steady

"O God my heart is fixed." (Psalm 108:1a)

Everything around us is changing at a frightening, disorienting speed. Stay steady. Fix your heart on Jesus. Fix your heart on the Word of God and do not move one inch away from the truth of it, no matter what culture says, no matter what friends say, no matter what some "evangelical" teachers are now saying. "And wisdom and knowledge shall be the stability of your times." (Isaiah 33:6) Where does that wisdom and knowledge come from? The Word of God. Abandon even one portion of it at your own peril.

Stay steady as an oak, stay true to His truth, do not be moved no matter how furiously the storm of lies blows around you. "Heaven and earth will pass away, but my words will never pass away.) (Matthew 24:35)

Make His Word the rock of truth on which you stand.

# October 24th

## Let Him Choose

"and he gave them their request, but since leanness into their souls." - Psalm 106:15.

God will eventually let you have what you want, even if it is totally out of his will. I've consistently seen this in pursuing a relationship with an unbeliever. But the price you pay will be spiritual starvation and sidetracking His calling for you.

Let him choose for you, for he always chooses the best.

# October 25th

## Salt and Light

"Egypt was glad when they departed." Psalm 105:38

Whoever believes the idea that the world and unbelievers are happy when Christians are around hasn't read the scriptures or history. We bring salt and light. Salt stings and light can hurt the eyes of those in darkness. We also bring love and hope, truth and mercy and salvation in Jesus. But make no mistake, most are happy when we leave or are silenced. Only those who will come to believe in Jesus will be glad we crashed the party.

# October 26<sup>th</sup>

## Drawing Near

"Draw nigh unto my soul, and redeem it." - Psalm 69:18

Many of us want God to deliver us and change us and break the sins that so cruelly bind us.

The answer is not in more books or how to's. It is drawing close to God and asking him to draw close to your soul, and His promise is to redeem us from all that binds us. Spending time with Jesus in His holy presence will bring deliverance from all our besetting sins.

"Draw near to God and He will draw near to you." (James 4:8)

# October 27th

## Serving

"So Elisha turned back from him, and took a yoke of oxen and slaughtered them and boiled their flesh, using the oxen's equipment, and gave it to the people, and they ate. Then he arose and followed Elijah, and became his servant." (1 Kings 19:21)

If you wish to be an Elijah, you must first be an Elisha. Serving others from the heart, and serving Jesus with all your heart - without thanks, recognition or concern for it - are absolute prerequisites for true greatness in His Kingdom. There is no room for ambition to be an Elijah if you are not willing to serve as an Elisha.

# October 28th

## Storm

"And they came to him, and awoke him, saying, Master, master, we perish. Then he arose, and rebuked the wind and the raging of the water: and they ceased, and there was a calm." Luke 8:24

Slow down…God is in complete control. Don't fear other people's fear, nor be stirred up to panic by other people's panic. Be calm in the storm, for Jesus is the Lord of the storm.

# October 29<sup>th</sup>

## So Soon

"Now also when I am old and greyheaded, O God, forsake me not; until I have shewed thy strength unto this generation, and thy power to every one that is to come." Psalm 71:18

So soon it is over,
The laughter, the tears that we share together,
These wonderful years...
Why do we waste them,
The days God has planned?
They run through our fingers,
Like grains of falling sand.
-Audrey Mieir-

# October 30<sup>th</sup>

## Stay

"Then they drew near to the village where they were going, and He indicated that He would have gone farther. But they constrained Him, saying, "Abide with us, for it is toward evening, and the day is far spent." And He went in to stay with them." - Luke 24:28-29

Two disciples were walking on the road after the resurrection, but they were filled with doubt and fear. A stranger came up to them and began to talk with them.

Their eyes were prevented from knowing that it was Jesus. Jesus explained all the Scriptures concerning himself and how these things had to take place.

Jesus looked like he was going to go in another direction, and you can hear the longing in their hearts: please, stay with us. The day is almost over and it's getting dark. And he stayed with them and showed them that it was He, Jesus, The risen Lord.

I am always greatly moved by this passage, because I know we often feel that the day is getting dimmer around us, and the night is quickly falling.

Yes, Lord, we believe in you and we believe your word is true. But the night is falling, and human fear wants to grip our hearts. But the words you speak to us cause our hearts to burn within us, with love for you and with eternal hope. Stay with us, Jesus, because the night is near.

And we hear Your precious words, "Never, ever will I leave you. Never, ever will I forsake you."

So let the night come. For you are with us Jesus, and it is enough.

# October 31$^{st}$

## Preparation

"Study to show thyself approved unto God, a workman that needeth not to be ashamed, rightly dividing the word of truth." 2 Timothy 2:15

David was anointed long before he got his moment. Don't jump the gun. Be spiritually fit and prepared when the moment comes so that pride and immaturity do not shipwreck you. Wait for His timing. Preparation is everything.

# November 1st

## The Way

"And the soul of the people was much discouraged because of the way." (Numbers 21:4)

Early Christians were called people of "The Way" or followers of "The Way." Jesus said, "I am the Way." Being a Christian - following Jesus - is both a relationship with Jesus and a walk on the road to Forever.

God's people sometimes can become discouraged because of the way; it can be hard. It can be baffling. It can be heartbreaking.

But God's Way is always true, whether we trust it or not; always good, even if it feels bad; and always leads to greater blessing and freedom, though there are obstacles along that Way. Trust Him. He IS the Way, He has made the Way, and He will show you how to walk in His Way.

He will never fail you or abandon you on the wayside.

# November 2<sup>nd</sup>

## Come Lord Jesus

"And the Spirit and the bride say, Come. And let him that heareth say, Come. And let him that is athirst come. And whosoever will, let him take the water of life freely." Revelation 22:17

Come Lord Jesus come
Come for all the injured lambs
Come for all the broken toys
Come for all the stolen girls
Come for all the shattered boys
Come Lord Jesus come
Come and end the suffering
Come and make right everything
Come and mend the broken heart
Come and mend the torn apart
Come Lord Jesus come
Come and dry each lonely tear
Come and calm each awful fear
Come Lord Jesus we need you so
Deliver those bowed so low
Who cry for love who feel alone who find a street and call it home for special kids afraid to be, come Lord Jesus, set them free...
Come Lord Jesus come.

# November 3$^{rd}$
## Boldly

"Let us therefore come boldly unto the throne of grace, that we may obtain mercy, and find grace to help in time of need. "Hebrews 4:16

God tells us to come boldly to His throne of Grace, not because we are worthy, but because we are needy. Do not hesitate on the way for fear of rejection, or a stranger will meet you to convince you that you are unworthy to come. Run to Jesus' arms. Dawdling will bring defeat. Don't talk to strangers on the way Home.

# November 4$^{th}$
## It Is Well

"It is well." 2 Kings 4:26.

Faith proclaims it even when your grief is beyond words and hope seems gone. Because God is always good and His love never fails us.

# November 5<sup>th</sup>
## All Our Days

"Asa's heart was loyal to the Lord all his days." 1 Kings 15:14

We thank God for the grace of Jesus that cleanses us from all sin and continues to cleanse. We are grateful for the grace that sustains us in all hard times, and the mercy that picks us up and restores us when we fall.

But in each of our hearts, there is a longing, a cry that says, "Lord despite my weaknesses and failures, let me remain loyal to You all the days of my life."

God grant that whatever comes, we will never abandon the One that gave all so we may one day hear, "Well done, good and faithful servant." God give us that grace.

# November 6<sup>th</sup>
## Faith

"Now faith is the substance of things hoped for, the evidence of things not seen." Hebrews 11:11

Faith is putting a thumbtack of confidence in the promise of God's Next for your life on the other side of painful circumstances.

# November 7<sup>th</sup>
# Working Out

"Wherefore, my beloved, as ye have always obeyed, not as in my presence only, but now much more in my absence, work out your own salvation with fear and trembling." Philippians 2:2

"Work out your own salvation with fear & trembling." It literally means, "Make yourself fit for." If we spent at least as much time or more on our spiritual workouts in God's gym as we do in human ones, we would be spiritual superheroes.

# November 8<sup>th</sup>
# Better Than Me

"Let each esteem other better than himself."(Philippians 2:3

Today I'm going to look at everyone I meet and say to myself, "you're better than me." It's a hard command in a world that says love yourself and put yourself first. But for us, it produces a humility of heart that I believe melts conflicts and produces godly love. I cannot do this on my own, but through Him, I can. I am commanded to and by His grace, I will. Besides, who am I? I have nothing - and am nothing - except what He gave me and made me be. I take pride in Him. Not in me.

# November 9th
# What If?

"And when they found them not, they drew Jason and certain brethren unto the rulers of the city, crying, These that have turned the world upside down are come hither also;" Acts 17:6

What if the printers broke and we couldn't print the bulletin? And someone forgot the PowerPoint for the songs and the message? And what if the sound system fried or the power went out, and the instruments were missing, and the volunteers could not come; what if all you had was a Cross behind you and a Bible in front of you, neither notes nor assistants nor a schedule nor a sound system nor a projector; could we still "do church?" A challenging thought in a technologically advanced and highly scripted church age.

The Apostles had only the cross and the scriptures. With them, they turned the world upside down.

# November 10<sup>th</sup>
## Prophets

"Thus saith the Lord of hosts, hearken not unto the words of the prophets that prophesy unto you; they make you vain; they speak a vision of their own heart, and not out of the mouth of the Lord." (Jeremiah 23:16)

We need to be cautious of a lot of the modern prophets who tell us how big our ministries are going to be, how anointed we are, and how much we are going to prosper. True prophecy from God humbles us, challenges us, and gives us clear and precise direction and correction from the Lord. It doesn't stroke our pride and make us vain as this scripture says. beware of prophets who always prophesy smooth things.

# November 11<sup>th</sup>
## Seeking

"...but stand still a while, that I may show you the Word of God." (1 Samuel 9:27b)

God is seeking those who above all else are willing to stand still and seek Him in His Word. This is not the misinterpretation of the "be still" scripture that many teachers use as a call to some new prayer method requiring breathing methods and repetitions of words but rather an active, deliberate delay of all daily activity for a time to focus on God's Word in prayer. If you seek, you will find, and God is looking to raise up a generation that will SEEK HIM with all of their hearts - in His Word. May God give us the discipline and grace to shut out the world and the many voices today for a time and just open His Word that we may behold wondrous things out of it. (Psalm 119:18) "This is the generation of them that seek Him...(Psalm 24:6a)

# November 12<sup>th</sup>
## Beware

"Beloved, believe not every spirit, but try the spirits whether they are of God: because many false prophets are gone out into the world." 1 John 4:1

Beware of prophecies that sound like they were taken from a Chinese fortune cookie.

# November 13<sup>th</sup>
## Entertainment

"Redeeming the time, because the days are evil."
Ephesians5:16

It's time for the churches in the west to take off the emcee clothes, the clown outfits, the corporate suits and the entertainment and social butterfly gowns and suit up with their armor. It's the only thing that is befitting His warriors. Redeem the time while it is still daylight. Get ready. The battle is on us, and Jesus is not far behind.

# November 14<sup>th</sup>
## Reflection

"And when he thought thereon, he wept." (Mark 14:72b)

Part of why we don't change as believers is because we don't take the time to sit with Jesus and His Word and think and listen. Living a Psalm 139:23-24 life requires reflection, time, and yes, tears. Search me, O God...

# November 15<sup>th</sup>
## God's Image

"But He perceived their craftiness, and said to them, "Why do you test Me? Show Me a denarius. Whose image and inscription does it have?" They answered and said, "Caesar's." And He said to them, "Render therefore to Caesar the things that are Caesar's, and to God the things that are God's." (Luke 20:23-25).

The money had Caesar's image engraved in it. It belonged to him. You have been made with God's image engraved in you, in your very DNA. Give Him what bears His image - your whole life. Give to God what is His. "For you are bought with a price: Therefore glorify God in your body and spirit, which are God's. (1 Cor. 6:20)

# November 16<sup>th</sup>
## Rejoicing

"Not that I speak in respect of want: for I have learned, in whatsoever state I am, therewith to be content." Philippians 4:11

Paul did two things all through his life and calling: He rejoiced and was content no matter what his circumstances, in prison, through shipwreck and everything else: And, he took advantage of every circumstance in order to preach the Gospel and bring others to Jesus, whether imprisoned or shipwrecked. God, give me the heart to rejoice in the midst of any and ALL circumstances, and the focus to use those circumstances, no matter how hard, to lead others to Jesus.

# November 17<sup>th</sup>
## Garment of Truth

"Sanctify them through thy truth: thy word is truth." John 17:17

God's truth in scripture is like an intricately woven garment. If you are foolish enough to pull out and discard one thread, the whole fabric of truth will unravel in your life till you are left with nothing of truth at all, but covered with a new garment of deception & lies.

# November 18<sup>th</sup>
# Homesick

"For here have we no continuing city, but we seek one to come." Hebrews 13:14

Not an original thought, but one of the realities of heaven to come for me is that, contrary to what unbelievers would think, it's not times of suffering and pain when we long for heaven. For me, it's on a stunningly beautiful day, when all is well, and all my senses are filled with life and awe at this beautiful creation; it is then that I long most for heaven. It is then that I know all of this is just a taste of That. It is then I know heaven is not an escape for the weak. It is Home for the homesick Pilgrim.

# November 19<sup>th</sup>
# Blocked

. "Surely he shall deliver you from the snare of the fowler, and from the noisome pestilence." Hebrews 13:14

"Jesus, for the block."

Are you going through a time when you are feeling battered on every side by the enemy? Psalm 91 is a great comfort. "Surely he shall deliver you from the snare of the fowler, and from the noisome pestilence." Noisome means a chasm, a calamity. But, "He shall cover you with His feathers, and under His wings will you trust." "Cover" means to block, overshadow, screen, stop the approach, shut off.

When the enemy is opening up a chasm of attacks in front of you, just let Jesus pick you up and snuggle you into His feathers. He's going to block the enemy, stop His approach and shut Him off. Nestle into the Father. He will keep you covered. He knows how to block the attacks and keep you safe in His protective love.

# November 20<sup>th</sup>
## Soldiers

Thou therefore endure hardness, as a good soldier of Jesus Christ. 1 Timothy 2:3

God needs soldiers in this hour who have been fed on the lean mean diet of the truth of God's Word and have no moral uncertainty as to who our enemy is and what they need to do to engage and defeat him.

# November 21ˢᵗ
## Landmines

"Are they ministers of Christ? (I speak as a fool) I am more; in labors more abundant, in stripes above measure, in prisons more frequent, in deaths oft. Of the Jews five times received I forty stripes save one. Thrice was I beaten with rods, once was I stoned, thrice I suffered shipwreck, a night and a day I have been in the deep; In journeyings often, in perils of waters, in perils of robbers, in perils by mine own countrymen, in perils by the heathen, in perils in the city, in perils in the wilderness, in perils in the sea, in perils among false brethren; In weariness and painfulness, in watchings often, in hunger and thirst, in fastings often, in cold and nakedness. Beside those things that are without, that which cometh upon me daily, the care of all the churches." 1 Corinthians 11:23-28

I wish we could divest ourselves of the Pollyanna view of ministry that it's an easy ride filled with perks. Real ministry is a Humvee hitting potholes trying to avoid landmines.

# November 22$^{nd}$
## Fearful

"God has not given us a spirit of fear but of power, love, and of sound mind." 2 Tim. 1:7.

We are living in fearful times. But God forbid that we should become fearful people!

# November 23<sup>rd</sup>
## Preparation

"O house of Israel, cannot I do with you as this potter? saith the Lord. Behold, as the clay is in the potter's hand, so are ye in mine hand, O house of Israel." Jeremiah 18:6

Preparation requires cooperation. If you want God to use you, you need to let Him mold you, break you, and make you into a vessel of honor. Don't curse your circumstances; bless the tools that God is using to make you more like Jesus.

# November 24<sup>th</sup>
# Not Afraid

"Fear thou not; for I am with thee: be not dismayed; for I am thy God: I will strengthen thee; yea, I will help thee; yea, I will uphold thee with the right hand of my righteousness." Isaiah 41:10.

We are living in fearful times. But today God reminded me of this precious promise. He is with us!

# November 25<sup>th</sup>
# No Place

"Neither give place to the devil.'" Ephesians 4:27

The enemy is sly, lithe, deliberate, stealthy and cruel. He knows his strategy and your weaknesses. It's time to step up and surprise him by closing the doors to sin, dropping the weights and repairing our armor.

# November 26<sup>th</sup>
# Draining Resources

Elisha's servant Gehazi lied to both Naaman and Elisha in order to enrich himself. Elisha's response: "Is it a time to receive money, and to receive garments, and oliveyards, and vineyards, and sheep, and oxen, and menservants, and maidservants?" (2 Kings 5:26b)

In the same way that Gehazi received the leprosy that God had just healed from Naaman - because of his greed - those who are draining the body of Christ of precious resources which are so needed to reach the lost, especially overseas, for their own enrichment and personal gain will, when our own economic hard times come, be rejected, disqualified and treated as lepers by those that they have used to further their own lavish lifestyles.

# November 27<sup>th</sup>
# Honorable

"Was he not most honorable of three? therefore he was their captain: howbeit he attained not unto the first three." (2 Samuel 23:19)

Even in Old Testament times, people were recognized by their success. That's human nature. Or as the saying goes, everyone loves a winner. Or as the purpose driven saying goes, "go with the go-ers or lose with the losers."

How gracious of God to remind us that many may not "attain" but are honorable. Much love this morning to my many friends and especially pastor/ministry folks (you know who you are!) who labor ceaselessly, love without return and give without asking anything back. You may not be an achiever according to worldly standards, but you are honorable, and mighty before God. Soldier on! Your reward is with Him, and heaven awaits your triumphant Homecoming where He will show you how much that you did, unrecognized, built great things for the Kingdom of God.

# November 28<sup>th</sup>
# Enduring Discipleship

It's so easy in ministry, particularly in youth ministry, to do all kinds of worldly-imitating-gimmicky things to attract a crowd. But as we are to be imitators of Christ and not the world, how useful really is all the "stink bait" we dangle out there? It's almost disingenuous; like, "Here are some Cracker Jacks. Oh, and there's a Jesus prize in the box, too..."

My heart's cry is that the Word, the presence and power of Jesus and His love will be all we need to do ministry.

In the end, it's not about who comes to the events - but who comes back, who stays, who ENDURES. Salvation is crucial, but discipleship is mandatory.

It's not about showing up to the Prom. It's about making it to the Reunion.

# November 29<sup>th</sup>
# His Battle

"The Lord will fight for you, and you will hold your peace." – Genesis 14:14

Whether in family, friendships or in the world, it is good to know that ultimately it is the Lord who fights our battles. It seems to be in our nature to jump in immediately to our own defense. A combative spirit doesn't glorify God. We are many times better if we simply hold our peace. If we are justified, God will be our defense.

# November 30<sup>th</sup>
# Enduring Words

"So Samuel grew, and the Lord was with him, and let none of his words fall to the ground." – 1 Samuel 3:19

Our world is filled with words. We talk much and listen little. It is a grace of God when we begin to weigh our words carefully, knowing that words matter, have weight and can have consequences for good and for bad.

My prayer is that our words will not fall to the ground and be forgotten as useless, hurtful or frivolous, but will befilled with the weight and power worthy of sons and daughters of the Living God. "Let the words of my mouth and the meditation of my heart be acceptable in thy sight, O Lord, my strength and my redeemer." Psalm 19:4

# December 1st
## Heaviness

"My soul melts from heaviness; strengthen me according to Thy Word." Psalm 119:28

There has never been a time that I have suffered and been bent low by heaviness that I have not found strength, power, comfort, and encouragement from picking up the precious Word of God and lingering there, long enough to let its healing balm sink down into every part of my aching heart. You can trust His Word, and you can trust this word, that in times of sadness and difficulty, His Word will give you all that you need to pick up and walk strong in the knowledge of His unwavering, unending care.

# December 2ʳᵈ
# Doing Good

"Do not grow weary in doing good." - 2 Thessalonians 3:13

I have a friend who likes to say, jokingly, "No good deed goes unpunished." It's funny, but reveals a discovery many who try to do good like Jesus make: their reward is with Him, and often the doing of good goes unrewarded here. More, it can be exhausting, because it takes us out of our routine and selfish world and causes us to extend ourselves in Jesus to those outside our circle of family and friends. Paul said not to grow weary in doing good. How? By daily refreshing ourselves at the feet of our Lord Jesus, basking in His presence and love, and feeding at the table of His precious Word. He will give you all the strength I need and wash all the weariness away, filling us anew with strength and power.

# December 3<sup>rd</sup>
# Climate Change?

"But the day of the Lord will come as a thief in the night; in the which the heavens shall pass away with a great noise, and the elements shall melt with fervent heat, the earth also and the works that are therein shall be burned up.

Seeing then that all these things shall be dissolved, what manner of persons ought ye to be in all holy conversation and godliness, looking for and hasting unto the coming of the day of God, wherein the heavens being on fire shall be dissolved, and the elements shall melt with fervent heat?

Nevertheless we, according to his promise, look for new heavens and a new earth, wherein † dwelleth righteousness. " 2 Peter 3:10-13

The message of the Gospel is not climate change. The Gospel is the message of sin, repentance, God's love, Jesus' sacrifice, being born again through turning away from our sins and old life - and the Great Hope, the return of Jesus Christ. Any other Gospel is not the Gospel at all. Wake up and read your Bible, friends. Jesus is coming back soon.

# December 4<sup>th</sup>
## Strengthened

"But David strengthened himself in the Lord his God."
1 Samuel 29:6

We all seek comfort and encouragement when we face difficult times and trying circumstances. Many are disappointed when they find friends, family and even pastors failing to provide what they seek.

Thank God for it. Learn like David to strengthen yourself in the Lord. It is important to fellowship and gain strength from each other in the Lord, but if you follow on, God will bring you into straits in which there will be no hand to guide but His, no comfort but His love. And there you will learn through spending time in His Word to strengthen yourself in Him. It is a strength that cannot be taken away, for it comes from the Lord Himself, who cannot fail.

# December 5<sup>th</sup>
## Invasion

"For it is a day of trouble, and of treading down, and of perplexity by the Lord GOD of hosts in the valley of vision, breaking down the walls, and of crying to the mountains."(Isaiah 22:5)

Walls, in the scriptures, always represent a defense against invasion. That picture is applicable in spiritual warfare, to us as a culture, and as individuals. When we begin to erase the boundaries of God's Word - when we begin to call that which is sin in God's eyes not sin - when we begin to ignore the plain and non-negotiable boundaries regarding occult practices, greed, substance abuse, sexual practices, and other clear scriptural principles - then we have set ourselves up for "a day of trouble and treading down, and crying." We have invited the enemy to invade, plain and simple. And while a godless society merely views these changes as "social evolution and enlightenment," Satan sees it as the open doors he needs to move his demonic troops into the land and begin to occupy both places and people.

# December 6<sup>th</sup>
## His Help

"For nothing restrains the Lord from saving by many or by few." – 1 Samuel 14:6

Jesus, help us to see the challenges and difficulties of our lives through Your eyes. You do the impossible. You healed the sick, raised the dead and cast out devils. How can we not trust You for all things, You who love us perfectly and works all things together for good for us?

Jesus, help us not to look at what we have, for we will always fall short of what we need to obtain victory. "What is it you have in your hand?" God asked Moses. (Exodus 4:2.) He replied that it was a rod; probably a simple staff or stick. Through that, in God's Hand, it became a tool to help bring deliverance to all of Israel.

What do you have in your hand? Give it to God, trust Him to do the rest, knowing that He is not restrained based on "many or few" but merely on a heart determined to trust Him in faith for all things.

# December 7th
# The Work of Sin

"For the wages of sin is death; but the gift of God is eternal life through Jesus Christ our Lord." Romans 6:23

The problem with sin is, what begins as ugly and repulsive to us - once it gains a foothold in our life – then becomes just uncomfortable, then as we indulge it repeatedly it becomes comfortable, then numbing, then needful, and finally, it is systemically ingrained. It begins to obliterate our personality and our identity. We can become our sin.

# December 8<sup>th</sup>
# No Part Dark

"Having no part dark." (Luke 11:36)

It IS possible. Jesus thinks it's important. It's cleanup time. By Your Spirit, Jesus.

# December 9<sup>th</sup>
# Outlast The Enemy

Wherefore take unto you the whole armor of God, that ye may be able to withstand in the evil day, and having done all, to stand. Ephesians 6:13

We must be determined to outlast the enemy and his attacks and to stand no matter what. Giving up under the attacks is never an option.

# December 10th
## Clarity

"For if the trumpet give an uncertain sound, who shall prepare himself to the battle? 1 Cor.14:8."

The battle is upon us. And the western church has lost the crystal clear clarity of the truth of the Gospel. We are not ready for the battle. Where are the Elijahs of God?

# December 11<sup>th</sup>
# Get Back Up

Knocked down, but not knocked out. Get back up when everything hurts and when your guts are screaming stop. Someone spike your leg when you just hit your stride again? Suck it up. Wipe off the blood and the mud, keep your eyes on the prize of the high calling in Jesus and run for the finish line. You preached it, now live it out. It's the real way of Jesus. That's the real "your best life now" - giving it ALL - surrendered to the call. No matter the pain, or the cost.

2 Cor. 4:8-10. 1 Cor. 9:24-27. Read it. Live it.

# December 12<sup>th</sup>
## All Means All

Matthew 19 thoughts...

The rich young ruler asked, "What good deed do I have to do to inherit eternal life?" Jesus said, "keep the commandments."

His question to Jesus: "Which ones?"

Moments later, Peter said, "We left everything and followed you. What then shall we have?"

I sometimes think these two questions are at the root of a lot of our struggles as believers. We ask,

- What's the least I have to do - what do I have to give up for Jesus?

- What's in it for me?

The answer is all, and a cross.

And in surrendering all and taking the cross, we inherit everything.

All means all.

I stand convicted this morning.

# December 13<sup>th</sup>
# Buy From Me

"I counsel thee to buy of me gold tried in the fire, that thou mayest be rich; and white raiment, that thou mayest be clothed, and that the shame of thy nakedness do not appear; and anoint thine eyes with eyesalve, that thou mayest see." Revelation 3:18

How do we "but" these things from Him who paid it all for us? Through prayer, through self-examination Psalm 139-stule, through repentance when we fail, through disciplined time in the Word of God, and from a heart that, by His grace, loves Him with all we are.

# December 14<sup>th</sup>
## Praying Through

"And he said, I will not let thee go, except thou bless me.Genesis 32:26b

We have lost the discipline of "praying through." It was once said wisely that prayer will change THINGS or prayer will change YOU. Either way, God answers. So you pray until things change, or until His peace that passes understanding rules in your heart and mind that says, "God has heard me." And like Daniel, the answer may be days in coming. But you "pray through." How do you know when you're "through?" You pray until something breaks in the Spirit. You'll know. Pray with the fervor of Jacob: "Lord, I'm not letting go until I know we've met here..." The kingdom suffers violence, and the violent take it by force. God loves determined pray-ers. May God give us a fiery heart that is willing to "pray through"!

# December 15th
# Prayer Strategy

"Bless those who curse you, pray for those who despitefully use you." Matthew 5:44

Realtime spiritual warfare prayer strategy when under attack by the wicked one (or if he is using others to be his attackers): RESCIND, REVOKE AND REBUKE every evil attack in prayer. But never, ever return a curse.

And NEVER receive the enemy's attack passively. Remember the 3 Rs of spiritual warfare!

# December 16<sup>th</sup>

## Written On Our Hearts

Exodus 28:9-12.

The priests had two stones, with the names of the 12 sons of Israel, placed on their shoulders.

Isn't that the heart of true Pastoral ministry? Their names – the names of those God gives you to care for and carry – written on your heart, their burdens carried on your shoulders in prayer.

# December 17th
# Battle Well

"For this purpose the Son of God was manifested, that he might destroy the works of the devil." (1 John 3:9)

We are His hands and His feet in this world. Let us put our hands to the war, and battle well for the sake of Jesus and the ones He died to set free.

"Let God arise, and the enemy be scattered!" (Psalm 68:1)

# December 18<sup>th</sup>
## Not Just Words

"For the Kingdom of God is not in word but in power." – 1 Corinthians 4:20

When people are hurting, it is easy to want to just rush in and make it stop. We are well-intentioned but often end up relying on well-worn expressions (aren't you glad your loved one is with Jesus now?) (You just need to trust God.)

It's often the last thing they need to hear.

But when the words are said, what they need more than anything is for God's power to intervene, to give them strength, to give them hope, and yes, to do miracles. Let's not limit the Holy One of Israel by giving words but not praying in the power of God for hurting hearts.

# December 19<sup>th</sup>
## Clean

When Jesus filled the boat with fish, Peter said,
"Depart from me, for I am a sinful man, O Lord."
In our ordinary days, we can put God in an "alternate
universe" in which He stays there, and we can stay here. It's
almost like having a family member in the next room, but
your door is locked, like kids growing up with parents.

But when Jesus crashes through the door by the power
of the Spirit and does miracles, we're hit full force with the
light crashing into our dark room, we're struck by how
utterly unholy, and unlike Him in our flesh we are…and
our first response is, "Go away, I'm unclean!"

But He comes to bring us out of our dark room into
His light. Let go of the darkness and sin. He will make you
clean.

# December 20<sup>th</sup>
# Burning

"The Lord appeared to him in a flame of fire from the midst of a bush. And the bush burned with fire, but the bush was not consumed." (Ex. 3:2)

You may fear healing means giving up what is familiar to you, fear that God will change you into something cold, fearing holiness is confining, empty and lifeless. But our God, a consuming Fire, burns but does not destroy, burning the things that destroy you but not destroying YOU. You don't lose your identity - you find it!

# December 21ˢᵗ
# Choosing to Suffer

"May the King live forever! Why should my face not look sad when the city where my fathers are buried lies in ruins and its gates have been destroyed by fire?" – Nehemiah 2:3

Nehemiah, born in exile, knew nothing of the wars that destroyed their homeland, except for what he'd heard. He moved up through the political ranks to a place right next to the king – totally trusted – totally provided for. Why leave that?

Perhaps it struck him: "Hey, I'm in a position to do something!" But it was what he did that is so astonishing. He didn't send a monthly tithe to the exiles. (He was probably doing that already.) He gave up his life of privilege to do something himself. Can you imagine?

God can use a heart like that.

He left everything – for nothing.

He traded a palace for rubble.

That's commitment!

# December 22$^{nd}$
# Reproach

"What you are doing is not good. Should you not walk in the fear of God because of the reproach of the nations, our enemies?" – Nehemiah 5:9

The world will mock us, whether we are living right or not. But why give them ammunition? We can engage in worldly sins and activities with our old non-Christian friends who know that we are Christians, and they smile. We think, "Oh, I want them to know that I am an ok person. I can still party with them and cuss and have a good time/ I can relate to them." They smile because they know we're phony. We're no different than them, and we just proved it.

The world doesn't respect us when we bend over backward to be like them. They expect us to be different. You can't save a drowning man if you get in the water and let them pull you over.

We do live in a glass house. Once you come to Jesus, you're under the world's microscope, waiting for you to prove you are not real and not faithful to your God. But on a deeper level, many are dying, scared, and desperately hoping you are for real.

Let's do all we can to walk in the fear of God for the sake of those who need Jesus to pull them out of the darkness.

# December 23<sup>rd</sup>
## Guard

"But we prayed to our God and posted a guard night and day to meet this threat." – Nehemiah 4:9

Satan never gives up. He is more determined than you know, and I believe the closer we get to the end, the more viciously and cruelly he will attack because he knows his destruction is coming. I don't think he is so blind that he thinks that he will win. I think, like the insane Hitler in his final days, Satan's goal has gone from winning to "destroy everything."

You're at the top of that list. You're marked and targeted. Deal with it, live with it and prepare for it. And do not fear it! "Our God shall fight for us." Nehemiah 4:20b

# December 24<sup>th</sup>
## Separation, One

"You have not kept the charge of My holy things. But you have set foreigners to keep charge of my sanctuary." – Ezekiel 44:8

One of the great responsibilities of pastors, leaders and other mature believers in the church is to guard the sacred things of God: The Word, worship, fellowship, communion. More and more in this present church age, we are allowing "foreigners" to keep charge – in other words, mixing secular songs with Christian worship, allowing secular humanistic precepts to be taught from the pulpit, letting unbelievers even lead worship. The charge of the sanctuary cannot be given over to the secular. We cannot allow strange fire on His altar, no matter how we may deceive ourselves into thinking it's going to attract the lost. Though it may appeal to their flesh, it is a mixed stream and will take the power out of the true life-changing Gospel of Jesus. Keep the house of God free from the world.

# December 25<sup>th</sup>
## Separation, Two

"They shall teach My people the difference between the holy and profane, and cause them to discern between the unclean and the clean." – Ezekiel 44:23

We live in such a compromised age that many believers go to R-rated movies, watch contaminated comedies and television shows, and participate in worldly parties and activities not ever letting others even suspect that we are believers. Yet the Bible calls for us to "Come out from among them and be ye separate." It does not mean that we do not be with unbelievers, to reach unbelievers. But we are told to separate ourselves from the THINGS of the world. If young believers have learned by our example, have they learned to discern between the clean and the unclean, that which is allowable and that which is ruinous to their spiritual walks? Let us as parents, pastors and leaders be diligent to teach them to know, that they might be an example – not of shady compromise – but of outstanding, shining light.

# December 26<sup>th</sup>
# Our Possession

"And you shall give them no possession in Israel. I am their possession." Ezekiel 44:28

Of all the tribes, only the Levites had no property or possessions on this earth to call their own. God calls us a kingdom of priests to Himself. It is not meant to be a walk of deprivation and sorrow; we are never taught to seek after worldly possessions. If they come, we must use them for His sake, enjoy them because He gave them, but never make them either a goal nor a craving. All of it passes away. Blessed are they who cling wholly to Jesus Himself, and are content to let Him be their possession, their portion, their all.

# December 27<sup>th</sup>
# Contending

"...it was needful for me to write to you, and exhort you that you would earnestly contend for the faith which was once delivered unto the saints." - Jude 1:4b

To contend is to defend or fight for. I am continually grieved at the weak and powerless nature of our modern presentation of the gospel. We are so afraid of offending people, we are so eager to please people and to give them a message that makes them happy and make us socially relevant that we end up not defending the faith, but apologizing for it, taking the edges off of it and putting an attractive outfit on it so we can get people in the door. This is not and has never been the Gospel. We have been entrusted with dynamite - "dunamis" - the power of the Holy Spirit of the living God, not puppies and pancakes. I am praying for an unleashing of that power on a godless and desperate culture, and for spines for young men and women of God who will proclaim truth without the fear of man causing them to soften the message and thus take away its power to redeem from sin and death.

# December 28th
## Resting Place

"My people have been lost sheep. They have gone from mountain to hill; they have forgotten their resting place." – Jeremiah 50:6

In our times, everything and everyone around us seems to need our attention. And we get weary. There are books and seminars and messages about how to avoid burnout, but they fail to provide the one thing we need most – a resting place. For us as believers, we can also reach burnout, and for those in ministry, it can be especially easy. We must always remember that the thing we need to strive for is to "strive to enter into His rest," and in His resting place, we shall find rest and peace, and refreshment to face any challenge ahead.

# December 29<sup>th</sup>
## Hedged In

"He has hedged me in so I cannot get out." – Lamentations 3:7

There are times in our walk with Jesus that He deems it necessary to "hedge" us in – to remove things we lean on, to curtail activity, to shake up relationships outside our family, to block opportunities and to thwart our human plans. Why does He do this? Is this a sign He is displeased, that we have somehow lost our relationship with God? Far from it. God usually hedges us because our need to totally rely on Him, His will, His guidance, grace, and love require we "come away" with our Beloved for a time removed from every distraction.

There we learn to trust in only Him, to love Him more fully and to lean on Him completely.

Are you hedged in? Thank Him for the extreme love that has drawn you aside so He may say, "You are mine," and you will come up out of the wilderness, leaning on the arm of your Beloved. (Song of Songs, 8:5)

# December 30<sup>th</sup>
## Power of God

"When He had stopped speaking, He said to Simon, 'Launch out into the deep and let down your nets for a catch.' But Simon answered and said to Him, 'Master, we have toiled all night and caught nothing; nevertheless at Your Word I will let down the net.' And when they had done this, they caught a great number of fish, and their net was breaking. So they signaled to their partners in the other boat to come and help them. And they came and filled both the boats, so that they began to sink. When Simon Peter saw it, he fell down at Jesus' knees, saying, "Depart from me, for I am a sinful man, O Lord!" - Luke 5:1-5

When Jesus filled the boat with fish, Peter said, "Depart from me, for I am a sinful man, O Lord."

On ordinary days, we can put God in an "alternate universe" in which He stays there, and we can stay here. It's almost like having a family member in the next room, but your door is locked, like kids when they are growing up with their parents.

But when Jesus crashes through the door by the power of the Spirit and does miracles, we're hit full force with the light crashing into our dark room, and we're struck by how utterly unholy and unlike Him in our flesh we are…and our first response is, "Go away, I'm unclean!"

But He comes to bring us out of our dark room into His light. Let go of the darkness and sin. He will make you clean.

# December 31ˢᵗ
## His Word

"Thy Word is a lamp unto my feet, and a light unto my path." (Psalm 119:115)

I close this volume of devotionals with a word from my heart. God's Word is the dearest treasure I own on this earth. All my possessions you may take, but I must have that Book. In my first days with Him, I devoured it like a starving man. My second Bible became tattered and fell apart after a year from the reading and the underlining. I do not boast in saying that. I simply was so needy that I could not have lived without that much of His dear Word. And I am thankful that it became daily bread. The many and awful storms I have faced in my 28 years with Him would have drowned me and destroyed me without that Word. In many confrontations with unbelievers and demon-infested lost souls, I would have been torn apart without that Word, hidden in my heart, that suddenly poured from my lips and brought Power and Life. I write this, and this book, with a burning prayer that you too will devour His Word with all you have, and never take it for granted. No earthly gift will ever equal the one you are privileged to read every day - His Holy Word!

# ODDS AND ENDS

## Salome

The spirit of Salome is rising up in this hour and seeking to silence the voice crying in the wilderness, "prepare the way of The Lord, and repent of your sins give your life to Jesus and be saved." First comes widespread and increasingly vile ridicule. Then, "off with their heads" - the only way to really silence the disturbing and inconvenient voice of conviction. and truth.

For those with ears to hear.

Time to stop apologizing for "the church" and be the VOICE.

## Proclaim

We are called to proclaim, not to explain. Those who have made up their minds not to believe in God will not be convinced by a mountain of evidence.

## Organic

True godly leadership is not knowing how to do the mechanics of ministry but how to walk in the heart of Jesus. It's organic, not mechanic.

## Gossip

Gossip is a weapon of crass destruction.

# The Cure

The problem is sin. The answer is Jesus. The cross is the deliverance. The resurrection is the hope. Everything else is a band aid.

# Upper Room

It is time to stop babysitting and start boot-camping our youth. We need to take them from the romper room to the upper room. This is a war, not a video game.

# Worship

Worship is really the bleating of God's sheep crying for their Shepherd...

# Night Watches

In the deep night watches when sleep escapes me, my Father is always near. "For You, Lord, only make me to dwell in safety."

# More

The spiritual nature of God's people is that we tend toward spiritual deterioration. You know that about yourself. Don't you? You know we have to fight to stay fit, to stay strong, to grow. That is why "nice" messages are so dangerous- like junk food - all sugar, quick high, no nutrition. We need to be forever challenged toward MORE. My yearly fear is that on January 1st next year, I will be exactly the same as January 1st of this year.

# ABOUT THE AUTHOR

Gregory Reid is an ordained minister with American Evangelistic Association with an honorary doctorate from Logos Graduate School and is a retired Private Investigator. He has been a believer in Jesus since July 20th 1969, and has been in ministry since 1975. Over the years, Dr. Reid has been involved in crisis counseling, criminal justice training, overseas missions, media ministry, youth ministry and a number of other outreaches. His primary love and commitment is to youth ministry. He served as youth pastor at Crosspoint church in El Paso, Texas for 7 years and is currently speaking and preaching nationwide in many venues.

YouthFire
Box 370006
El Paso TX 79937
legendaryseeker@gmail.com
www.gregoryreid.com